The
CONTEMPORARY

Cookbook

The
CONTEMPORARY
COWBOY
Cookbook

RECIPES FROM THE WILD WEST TO WALL STREET

Photography by Mary Herrmann

DOTTY GRIFFITH

The
CONTEMPORARY
Cowboy Cookbook

From the Wild West to Wall Street

Lone Star Books
4720 Boston Way
Lanham, MD 20706

Distributed by
National Book Network

Library of Congress
Control Number: 2002111483

ISBN 1-58907-002-X (cl. alk. paper)

Printed in the United States.

Printed on acid-free paper (∞).

Book and cover design by Roxann L. Combs.

Photography by Mary Herrmann, unless otherwise indicated. Food styling by Lee Stanyer.

Photos on pages iii, xi, 1, 6, 9, 11, 13, 20, 21, 24, 61, 63, 73, 78, 83, 100, 106, 110, 125, 126, and 165 by PhotoDisc.

Photos on pages 62, 104, 106, and 120 by Corbis.

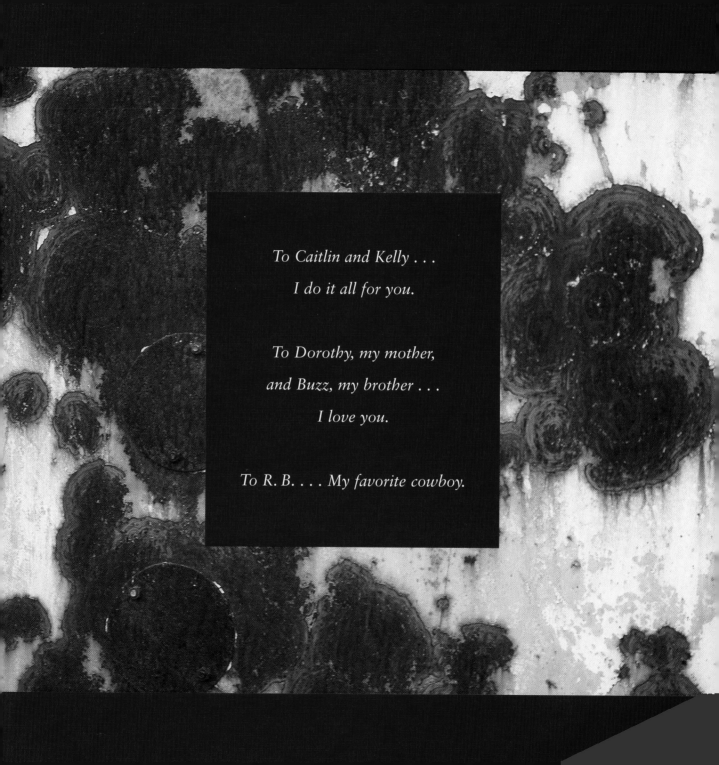

To Caitlin and Kelly . . .
I do it all for you.

To Dorothy, my mother,
and Buzz, my brother . . .
I love you.

To R. B. . . . My favorite cowboy.

CONTENTS

ACKNOWLEDGMENTS

Many thanks to all the cowboys who've given their time

and thought to this project; to those at Lone Star Books

whose efforts make my work look good;

to Martha Hershey for her recipe testing and camaraderie;

to my agent and friend Dedie Leahy for friendship and

encouragement no matter what; and to all who love the

cowboy lifestyle—however they choose to

express it—and their efforts to keep it alive.

INTRODUCTION

Being a cowboy—or loving one—is a bold statement. And you don't have to punch cattle or own a ranch to walk the walk and talk the talk. Of course, the trappings are part of the cowboy personality. Being a cowboy, however, is much more than a look. It is a way of thinking and acting.

While cowboys swagger, they also have a sensitive side. They're funny yet thoughtful, daring but mindful, rugged and also romantic. Most of all they're independent—totally unforgettable.

The contemporary cowboy's range doesn't have to be open. Today's cowboys can be found in corporate board rooms, courthouses, petroleum clubs, stock brokerages and high-tech labs.

Not all cowboys are men. From rodeos to real estate, women embody the "cowboy" way with determination, a distinctive personal style, a dry wit, and an indomitable mix of expertise and instinct. If Southern women are steel magnolias, then a cowboy woman is a cactus in bloom-beautiful and sharp.

Just as there is a cowboy way to look and act, there is a cowboy way of cooking and eating. Cowboy cuisine draws from all reaches of the cowboy world—chuck wagons, working ranch kitchens, suburban ranch-style three-two's, steak palaces, drive-ins, country cafes, and, of course, culinary temples where celebrity chefs wear boots. The fare is as appealing and as basic, yet inventive, as cowboys themselves.

The recipes in this book reflect contemporary cowboys—from corporate trail bosses, to rodeo riders, to wranglers who drive Mustangs, to "sho' nuf" ranchers—and the cooks—from the mommas, wives and partners, to the chuck wagon and penthouse chefs—who prepare the food they love.

The flavors and tastes represent all the regions—from the wild west to Wall Street—where the cowboy legend translates to contemporary men and women of character, achievement, sex appeal, and the rugged outdoors. Their lives are marked by bold strokes and independent action.

A PERSONAL NOTE

This is a fantasy cookbook—my personal fantasy of much land and many cattle. So many people have helped to fulfill this fantasy which began in my early childhood growing up in a small town called Terrell, Texas, near Dallas, spending weekends working cattle and pond fishing with my mom, dad and brother (Dorothy, Ed and Buzz) and my aunt and uncle, Clark and Nancy, on their respective ranches just outside of town.

Although my dad, a banker during the week, gave up punching cows on the weekends when I was fairly young and Brother Clark (as Daddy called him) moved his family away from ranch life to a small college town in Colorado the cowboy way remained a big part of my real—and imaginary—life.

As soon as I was tall enough to saddle a horse, Mom and Dad kept their promise to get me one—my beautiful Dinah, coal black with three white stockings and a white star on her forehead, and later, her colt, Cochise, a gray appaloosa. They were stabled in the barn behind grandmother Netsie Griffith's home. My "horsy" friends and I rode all over small-town Texas dirt roads. Instead of bikes, we rode horses to each others houses, up to the drive-in window at the Dairy Queen, and around town marauding neighbors' peach and plum trees.

Hardly a day went by when we didn't practice barrel racing, getting ready for the Lions Club-sponsored summer rodeo. For several years, Dad was the chairman of the rodeo. I was so proud the year he was in the officials' box looking on as Dinah and I won third place.

I often spent summers with my maternal grandparents, Monroe and Olga Koch, on their small ranch in New Ulm, an even smaller town about halfway between Austin and Houston. My grandfather

was also in the banking business. They kept a horse for me to ride, as well, and I spent many afternoons and weekends with my grandfather feeding cows and doctoring newborns. Heck, we even fixed fence.

Cattle auctions and rodeos—especially the Fort Worth Stock Show and Rodeo in February—are some of my fun memories. And throughout my life, fall weekends, along with Thanksgiving and Christmas holidays, have been spent on ranches where we leased hunting rights. The outdoors and hunting—dove, quail, white tail deer, and wild turkey—have been as much a part of my growing up as horses and cattle. And the two traditions merge for many cowboys as well.

Although I've worked and lived in Dallas since graduating from college, a big part of me remains grounded in the cowboy ways I grew up with. As a food journalist, I've enjoyed chronicling the rise of the cowboy chef, such as Grady Spears and Tim Love of Fort Worth, Dallas's Stephan Pyles founder of and father of New Texas Cuisine; with the Star Canyon restaurants in Dallas and Las Vegas; and Robert McGrath of the Roaring Fork restaurant in Phoenix. They've applied their extraordinary skills to create a sophisticated, yet earthy, style of cooking that never forgets the hard land and life it came from.

I grew up appreciating the simple cooking that makes the food of the West and Southwest so appealing. Touches of flavors and ingredients from Mexico, the South, the Plains, and the Rocky Mountains combine with those of the Indians, European settlers, and African American slaves in one of the earliest "fusion" cuisines.

The Contemporary Cowboy Cookbook celebrates my love of the Western lifestyle and the food that is so much a part of it.

REAL COWBOYS

The chuck wagon was the heart and soul of a trail drive. On the trail, men usually did the cooking—and a good trail cook made for happy cowboys. On the ranch, the cook house was as important as the corral. And it fell to the women—wives, mothers and sisters who were usually in charge of the kitchen—to feed the family and the cowboys that kept a ranch going. Again, the quality of the food was as important as good pay in keeping good help.

While on the trail, provisions were simple and selected because they traveled well—foods like cured meat, potatoes, canned peaches, flour and cornmeal, sugar, and, of course, beans. Wild game or fish and rare treats of wild fruit or vegetables were gathered along the way. Fresh beef was available from the stock on hand.

Staples on the ranch were a standard selection, although gardens could supplement a diet during the growing season and canning became a valued skill. Beef was, of course, plentiful. Variety came from wild game, along with farm-raised chickens, pigs, or goats.

Ranch fare is simple, but intense, food. The trick is to get the most flavor from the most basic of ingredients. A dish like chili—a meat stew flavored with chile peppers—is a prime example of flavor-dense cowboy fare. Whether prepared on the trail or in a modern kitchen, these recipes represent the backbone of the cowboy culinary repertoire.

SON-OF-A-BITCH STEW

2 POUNDS BEEF STEW MEAT,
  CUT INTO 1-INCH CUBES

½ CUP FLOUR

1 TEASPOON SALT OR TO TASTE

1 TEASPOON PEPPER OR TO TASTE

1 CUP CHOPPED ONION

2 CLOVES GARLIC, MINCED

2 TABLESPOONS BACON DRIPPINGS OR
  VEGETABLE OIL

2½ CUPS BEEF STOCK

1 TABLESPOON WORCESTERSHIRE SAUCE

4 CUPS POTATOES CUT INTO
  1-INCH CUBES

2 CUPS CARROTS, CUT INTO
  1-INCH THICK SLICES
  (OR EQUAL AMOUNT BABY CARROTS)

2 TABLESPOONS INSTANT DISSOLVING
  FLOUR OR 2 TABLESPOONS
  ALL-PURPOSE FLOUR STIRRED
  UNTIL SMOOTH INTO ¼ CUP WATER

The butchering of a steer for fresh meat was a culinary cause célèbre. Organ meats, such as heart, tongue, sweetbreads, kidneys, and marrow gut (the connective tissue between a cow's two stomachs), usually made their way into a Dutch oven for a concoction known as Son-of-a-Bitch Stew. Onions, maybe potatoes or carrots, might also be included. Bacon drippings were also used to brown the meat. Contemporary tastes might find a bubbling pot of organ meats a little hard to handle, so this stew just uses beef stew meat. But the technique and flavors are true to the simple tradition.

Place beef cubes into a plastic bag along with flour, salt, and pepper. Shake to evenly coat beef with seasoned flour. Shake off excess flour and set aside the beef. Place a large pot or Dutch oven over medium heat. Cook onion and garlic in bacon drippings or vegetable oil until onions begin to soften. Add beef cubes to pot and cook until beef browns, stirring occasionally.

Add stock and Worcestershire sauce. Bring liquid to a boil, reduce heat to simmer, cover, and cook gently for one hour. When beef is tender, add potatoes and carrots. Cook until vegetables are tender, easily pierced with a fork about 20–25 minutes. Add additional water to thin stew if too thick. Adjust seasoning to taste with salt and pepper.

To thicken stew, sprinkle instant dissolving flour over the stew, stirring constantly. Cook gently to thicken. Or stir all-purpose flour into water to make a smooth paste; stir in gradually and cook gently to thicken.

makes 4 to 6 servings

CHUCK WAGON CHILI

This is pretty basic stuff—a meat stew flavored with ground chile peppers, a few other spices and some tomato sauce for thickening. Dry spices and canned goods are about all you'd have in a chuck wagon larder. Works great with ground venison, as well as ground beef, since fresh venison doesn't take away from the herd and the final payout at the end of the trail.

Place ground meat in Dutch oven or large saucepan over medium heat. Cook until meat is no longer pink and liquid has evaporated. Do not brown too much.

Stir in chili powder, cumin, garlic, cayenne and oregano. Stir to coat meat evenly. Add tomato sauce and just enough water to cover meat. Bring liquid to a boil, reduce heat and simmer, covered, about 1 to 1½ hours until meat is tender. Stir in paprika and salt to taste.

Dissolve masa harina (a prepared mix for corn tortillas) or flour in 2 tablespoons water to make a smooth paste. Stir into chili until broth thickens and no lumps remain. Allow to simmer until desired thickness is reached. Adjust seasoning to taste.

- 2 POUNDS GROUND BEEF OR COARSELY GROUND BEEF OR VENISON FOR CHILI
- 3 TABLESPOONS CHILI POWDER
- 2 TEASPOONS GROUND CUMIN
- 2 TEASPOONS GRANULATED GARLIC
- 1 TEASPOON CAYENNE PEPPER OR TO TASTE
- 1 TEASPOON POWDERED OREGANO
- 1 8-OUNCE CAN TOMATO SAUCE
- 2 CUPS WATER OR AS NEEDED
- 1 TABLESPOON PAPRIKA
- 1 TEASPOON SALT OR TO TASTE
- 2 TABLESPOONS MASA HARINA OR INSTANT DISSOLVING FLOUR

makes 4 to 6 servings

8- TO 12-OUNCES LEAN BEEF OR VENISON

2 TABLESPOONS SOY SAUCE, OPTIONAL

½ TEASPOON SALT OR TO TASTE

½ TEASPOON PEPPER OR TO TASTE

1 SMALL ONION, CUT IN 2-INCH PIECES

6 CHERRY TOMATOES, OPTIONAL

1 SMALL GREEN BELL PEPPER, CUT IN
  2-INCH PIECES, OPTIONAL, OR
  4 WHOLE CANNED OR BOTTLED
  JALAPEÑO PEPPERS, HALVED, OPTIONAL

2 TABLESPOONS VEGETABLE OIL

makes 1 to 2 servings

STEAK ON A STICK

When dining under the stars, even the simplest preparation can be exquisite. This rustic meal-on-a-stick is a cowboy kebab that would work with beef or venison. Real cowboys on the range probably wouldn't have much more than salt, pepper, and maybe wild onions for seasoning. That'll do. You can add some flavor, however, with some soy sauce and a few extra vegetables.

Prepare coals for a medium hot fire. Meanwhile, cut meat into 2-inch cubes or into strips, 2 inches wide and ¼-inch thick. Place in a resealable plastic bag with soy sauce, shaking bag to evenly cover meat; set aside for 30 minutes to overnight.

Remove meat from soy sauce, shaking off excess. Season to taste with salt (go easy on the salt if meat has been marinated in soy sauce) and pepper. On 2 metal or water-soaked wooden skewers, thread the meat alternating with vegetable pieces. Brush lightly with oil.

When coals have burned down until covered with gray ash, place skewers on grill or secure in a grill basket for even easier handling. Cook 3 to 5 minutes on one side, then turn and cook 3 to 4 minutes longer, until meat is done to taste.

COWBOYS HAVE A *passion* FOR WHAT THEY DO.

IT ALL GOES BACK TO A *love of the land.*

BEING A COWBOY IS ALMOST A RELIGION—YOU'RE SO INHERENTLY

CLOSE TO *the Almighty* YOU DON'T HAVE TO GO TO CHURCH TO

APPRECIATE WHERE IT COMES FROM.

—Steve Murrin
West Fork Ranch,
Fort Worth, Texas

RANGE JERKY

*When there was too much to do to get back to the chuck
wagon, cowboys relied on the staple of plains Indians—dried
meat. Of course, Native Americans used venison or buffalo;
so did cowboys. Cowboys, however, also had access to beef and,
for them, jerky was more likely to be beef.*

*This recipe makes a tender jerky because it isn't likely to be
totally dry. The result is a more tender, flavorful jerky but it
won't keep as long in a cowboy's saddlebags. Store in an airtight
container for a week. For longer storage, freeze it.
Thaw and use as needed.*

2 POUNDS BONELESS VENISON HAM (LEG)
  OR BEEF BOTTOM ROUND

3 HEAPING TEASPOONS JUNIPER BERRIES

1 TEASPOON CAYENNE PEPPER OR
  TO TASTE

⅔ CUP BROWN SUGAR

2 TABLESPOONS COARSELY GROUND
  BLACK PEPPER

2 TABLESPOONS SALT

Rinse and dry venison or beef and freeze just until the meat is firm
enough to be sliced very thin, about 45 minutes to 1 hour. Slice as thin as
possible, no thicker than ⅛-inch, and cut slices into strips about 2 inches
wide. Set aside meat strips in a shallow pan.

While meat firms in freezer, combine juniper berries, cayenne pepper,
black pepper, brown sugar, and salt in a blender. Blend until well-mixed.

Rub spice blend into meat, evenly coating all sides. Place seasoned meat
strips directly on oven racks or on grill or cookie racks in the oven. Heat
oven to lowest setting (100° to 150°F) and dehydrate meat. This will take
8 to 12 hours. Shake off excess spices. Meat should be dry, tough and
stringy. Hey, it's jerky.

Store in an airtight container up to 1 week. For longer storage, place in
heavy-duty resealable plastic bags and freeze up to 3 months.

makes about 16 ounces
of jerky

12 CALF OR 16 LAMB TESTICLES OR
   2 CUPS TURKEY TESTICLES

1½ CUPS ALL-PURPOSE FLOUR

 1 TEASPOON BLACK PEPPER OR TO TASTE

 1 TEASPOON SALT OR TO TASTE

 ½ TEASPOON CAYENNE PEPPER

 2 CUPS VEGETABLE OIL FOR FRYING

makes 4 to 6 servings;
2 to 3 entree servings

ROUND-UP CALF FRIES

Whether you call them calf fries, or refer to them as mountain, Rocky Mountain or prairie oysters, these fries are a major treat on the range. Late spring and summer roundups were the time for gathering all the cows and calves and making steers out of most of the immature beeves. Lambs and goats meet the same fate about the same time each year, as well.

The byproduct of cutting or castrating the male calves, lambs, or turkeys was a "mess" (meaning a bunch) of testicles, ready for frying. These delicacies from a calf are about the size of small oysters, hence one of the euphemisms. The texture is almost ephemeral; they almost melt in the mouth as does foie gras. If you get a chance to sample calf, lamb, goat, or turkey fries, don't pass them up.

Using a sharp paring knife, cut and peel away the skin from the calf, lamb, or goat testicles. Because turkey testicles are so much smaller, use a sharp knife to pierce the external membrane to allow even cooking. Cut larger testicles in half so that all pieces are about the same size and will cook in the fryer in the same amount of time.

The organs are easier to handle if they are slightly frozen. If desired, cut the fries into bite-size pieces, about 1 inch. Pat dry with paper towels. Combine flour, pepper, salt, and cayenne in a plastic bag. Shake to combine dry ingredients.

Drop fries into seasoned flour a few pieces at a time. Shake off excess and set aside. Repeat until all pieces are coated. Meanwhile, heat oil in a deep skillet or fryer to 375°.

Drop fries into hot oil, a few pieces at a time. Cook, turning to brown on all sides, about 2 to 3 minutes or until golden. Drain on paper towels and keep warm until all pieces are fried. Serve with ketchup, salsa, steak sauce or cream gravy.

I'VE BEEN OFF THE *ranch* FOR 10 YEARS

BUT I CAN GO BACK AND KNOW EXACTLY WHAT TO DO.

A LOT OF PEOPLE DON'T UNDERSTAND *the rancher* AND

HIS *love for cattle and horses* AND HIS DESIRE TO BE A

HERDSMAN. ONE DAY SOMEONE ASKED ONE OF MY UNCLES

WHAT WE DO WITH OUR *time on the ranch* IN ALL THAT QUIET.

EDUCATED AT PRINCETON, HE WAS A PENSIVE FELLOW AND SAID,

"Sometimes I sit and think; sometimes I just sit."

ANSWERS LIKE THAT JUST DRIVE PEOPLE CRAZY

WHO DON'T UNDERSTAND.

—Alex Lassiter
Lassiter Ranch and Lassiter Grasslands Beef,
Matheson, Colorado

8 TO 10 FROG LEGS

1 CUP MILK OR EVAPORATED MILK

1 TEASPOON YELLOW MUSTARD

1 CUP FLOUR

1 TEASPOON SALT OR TO TASTE

½ TEASPOON BLACK PEPPER OR TO TASTE

1 TO 2 CUPS PEANUT OR OTHER MILD
VEGETABLE OIL FOR FRYING

LITTLE TANK
FROG LEGS

*Frog legs were undoubtedly a rare treat for cowboys.
First of all, big, fat bullfrogs from lakes or rivers are the frogs of
choice and watering holes were far and few between in most
areas of cowboy country. Second, it would take a lot of frogs to
feed a bunch of cowhands. No, frog legs were a "sport food"—
something you ate when you and a buddy had the time to spend
the better part of a night "gigging," which means hunting frogs
with a long-handled, two-pronged spear, around the edge of a
favorite pond or spring.*

*This is the way my mother, Dorothy Griffith, fried frog legs
when Ed, my dad, brought some home from the Little Tank on
the family GB Ranch. "Tank" is the Texas word for pond;
i.e., frogs from the small pond.*

Place frog legs in a shallow bowl or plastic bag. Add milk and mustard.
Stir or shake bag to evenly coat frog legs. Refrigerate for about an hour.

In a shallow bowl or a plastic bag, combine flour, salt, and black pepper. Remove frog legs from milk, allowing excess to drip away. Roll frog legs in flour or place in plastic bag one at a time and shake to coat evenly. Place frog legs on a sheet of wax paper so flour can adhere; let rest 10 to 20 minutes. For a thicker crust, dip frog legs in milk and flour a second time before allowing to dry.

Pour about 1 inch oil in a heavy bottom skillet and heat over medium high heat to about 350° to 375°. Carefully slide frog legs, one at a time, into hot oil. Do not crowd pan; sides should not touch. Cook 2 to 3 minutes or until brown on one side. Turn and cook until golden all over, about 5 to 6 minutes cooking time.

makes 3 to 4 servings

PAN-FRIED BREAM

*Where there are frogs, there are likely to be panfish,
either bream or crappie (freshwater perch), bass or catfish.
Catching a "mess" of fish meant a break from beef and bacon.*

Rinse fish and drain. Combine flour, cornmeal, salt, paprika, and pepper in a plastic bag. Shake bag to combine dry ingredients. Add fish fillets to bag one at a time and shake to coat evenly. Repeat until all fillets are coated; set aside.

Heat oil in a large skillet over medium heat to 350°. Add butter. Carefully slide fish into hot oil, 1 or 2 at a time. Fry 1 to 3 minutes per side (depending on thickness; freshwater fish fillets can be very thin) or until fish is golden and flakes easily with a fork. Drain on paper towels. Keep warm. Repeat until all fillets are cooked. Serve with ketchup, fresh lemon juice or tartar sauce.

2 POUNDS FISH FILLETS

¾ CUP FLOUR

⅓ CUP CORNMEAL

1 TEASPOON SALT OR TO TASTE

1 TEASPOON PAPRIKA

½ TEASPOON PEPPER OR TO TASTE

2 TABLESPOONS VEGETABLE OIL OR BACON DRIPPINGS

1 TABLESPOON BUTTER (OPTIONAL)

makes 6 to 8 servings

2 TO 3¼-INCH-THICK SLICES OF SALT PORK, RIND REMOVED

¼ CUP FLOUR OR AS NEEDED

1 TEASPOON BLACK PEPPER OR TO TASTE

1 TEASPOON OIL OR VEGETABLE COOKING SPRAY

½ CUP COFFEE

½ TEASPOON BROWN SUGAR OR TO TASTE, OPTIONAL

Substitute: *Pan-fry a thick slice of hamsteak and serve with Red-Eye Gravy as above.*

makes 1 serving

BATTER-FRIED SALT PORK *with* RED-EYE GRAVY

When times were lean on the range—and the daily menu consisted mainly of beans and bacon—putting a little batter on a piece of salt pork added culinary variety. Not much, but a little. Adding a splash of coffee to the pan made for a piquant gravy, providing still more relief for tired palates.

Dust the salt pork with flour. Sprinkle plenty of pepper on pork and rub the flour and pepper into the meat.

Heat a heavy-bottom skillet, preferably cast-iron, over medium heat. Add small amount of oil and swirl to coat the pan or spray with vegetable cooking spray. Cook salt pork until brown on one side, about 3 to 4 minutes; turn and brown other side. Remove from skillet and keep warm.

Stir in coffee and brown sugar, scraping to loosen any bits stuck to the bottom of the pan. Cook until liquid thickens slightly. Taste for seasoning. If needed, add salt, pepper, and additional brown sugar to taste. If gravy tastes too strong, thin with a splash of water.

When it comes to *food*, cowboys are

interested in the most efficient way

to get it from the *plate to the belly.*

On the range, there never was an

allotted *time* for dinner.

If you got to *stop and eat*, it was kind of special.

A typical cowboy meal was always

some kind of *meat* and whatever else

you could gather up.

When there wasn't any meat,

a *pot of beans* would do.

—*Steve Murrin*
West Fork Ranch,
Fort Worth, Texas

1 POUND DRY PINTO BEANS

2 CUPS CHOPPED ONION

2 CLOVES GARLIC, CRUSHED

3 TO 4 STRIPS BACON, CUT IN
1-INCH PIECES

1 FRESH JALAPEÑO, OPTIONAL

1 TEASPOON SALT, OR TO TASTE

makes 10 servings

1 CUP GRITS, QUICK-COOKING OR
OLD-FASHIONED (NOT INSTANT)

4 CUPS MILK OR 2 8-OUNCE CANS
EVAPORATED MILK PLUS 2 CUPS WATER

2 TABLESPOONS BUTTER OR AS DESIRED

1 TEASPOON SALT

1 3-OUNCE PACKAGE CREAM CHEESE OR
½ CUP MASCARPONE, OPTIONAL

1 TEASPOON SALT OR TO TASTE

½ TEASPOON PEPPER, OR TO TASTE

makes 8 servings

RANCHHAND
PINTO BEANS

*No chuck wagon is without a big pot of pinto beans.
A word about chili and beans, however. Beans are a side
with chili; put them in the chili if you want to,
just don't cook them together.*

Rinse beans in a colander. Place in a large saucepan or stockpot with enough water to cover. Soak overnight or place over high heat and bring to a boil. Cook for 1 minute. Turn off heat, cover and let beans soak for 1 hour.

When beans have finished soaking (either overnight or 1 hour in hot water), pour off soaking liquid. Rinse pot and return beans to pot. Add onions, garlic, bacon and enough water to cover by 1 inch. Add the jalapeño if you want the heat. Over high heat bring liquid to a boil. Then lower temperature, cover and simmer for 2 to 3 hours or until beans are tender. When beans are tender, add salt to taste.

CREAMY GRITS

*Although grits are more Southern than Western, a good many
cowboys with palates formed in the Deep South think a pot of
grits is as good as, maybe better than, potatoes—with a big pat
of butter or a ladleful of cream gravy. These are pretty fancied
up. The addition of cream cheese makes them even better.*

Combine grits, milk, butter, and salt over medium heat in a large saucepan. When milk begins to boil, lower heat. Simmer and stir over low heat, according to package directions: about 3 to 5 minutes for quick-cooking grits, 10 to 12 minutes for old-fashioned, or until thickened.

Remove from heat. If desired, stir in cream cheese, pepper, and more salt, if needed, to taste. Adjust texture with additional milk, if needed. May be made ahead, stored in refrigerator and reheated on top of stove over low heat.

FRIED POTATOES AND ONIONS

*Well-outfitted chuck wagons carried some potatoes
and onions just to spice things up. These taste great with just
about anything from eggs and bacon to a grilled steak.
By themselves, they're wonderful wrapped in a flour tortilla
with a generous spoonful of salsa. Bacon grease gives
them even more authentic flavor.*

4 MEDIUM RED POTATOES

1 TABLESPOON VEGETABLE OIL OR
BACON GREASE

½ CUP COARSELY CHOPPED ONION

1 TEASPOON SALT OR TO TASTE

1 TEASPOON PEPPER OR TO TASTE

Place potatoes in a medium saucepan over high heat with enough cold water to cover. Bring water to a boil, lower heat slightly, and cook until potatoes are easily pierced with a fork, about 15 minutes. Drain and allow to cool completely or refrigerate for several hours or overnight. Cut potatoes into 1-inch cubes and set aside.

Heat oil in a large skillet over medium heat. Add onions. Stir occasionally and cook until onions are wilted and begin to brown at the edges. Stir in potatoes. Cook, without stirring, until potatoes are brown on one side. Using a spatula to loosen potatoes, scrape the bottom of the pan and turn potatoes. Cook until brown. Season with salt and pepper to taste. Stir and serve immediately.

makes 4 servings

NOPALITOS

Green vegetables were hard to come by on the open range. Sometimes the tender inside of a prickly cactus leaf was about the only fresh, edible flora around. Long ago chuck wagon cooks probably would have loved to find nopalitos in a can or jar instead of having to peel off the tough exterior of a cactus. And they probably wouldn't have had fresh tomatoes, either. But take advantage of progress and enjoy these a simple, colorful way.

1 16-OUNCE CAN OR JAR OF NOPALITOS (READY-TO-EAT CACTUS LEAVES)

3 ROMA TOMATOES, OPTIONAL

3 TABLESPOONS FINELY CHOPPED ONION

½ CUP VEGETABLE OR EXTRA-VIRGIN OLIVE OIL

2 TABLESPOONS WHITE VINEGAR

½ TEASPOON SALT OR TO TASTE

¼ TEASPOON RED PEPPER FLAKES OR TO TASTE

1 TABLESPOON FRESH CILANTRO LEAVES

Empty nopalitos into a colander; rinse with water and drain well. Finely chop tomatoes and combine with drained nopalitos in a medium bowl along with chopped onion.

In a 1-cup measure, whisk together oil, vinegar, salt and red pepper flakes. Pour over nopalitos, mixing gently to coat evenly. Garnish with cilantro.

makes 4 to 6 servings

CRACKLIN' CORN BREAD

(OR HOT WATER CORN BREAD)

*You can't get more basic than fried corn meal mush.
Eat it for breakfast with butter and syrup or
with gravy at other meals. Sometimes when provisions
were low or time was tight, these could be the meal.*

Break larger pieces of crackling into smaller (½-inch) pieces; reserve. If using bacon, fry until crisp, drain and crumble into small pieces; reserve.

Combine cornmeal and salt in a large mixing bowl. Gradually stir in hot water and 2 tablespoons oil and mix until cornmeal takes up the liquid, adding just enough to make a moist, but firm batter, that will hold a shape.

Fold in cracklings or bacon and allow dough to cool enough to shape with your hands; omit cracklings or bacon for Hot Water Cornbread.

Scoop a heaping tablespoon of batter into the palm of one hand. Using both hands, shape the dough into a ½-inch thick oval patty. Place on wax paper. Repeat until all dough is formed into patties. Wet hands for easier handling.

Pour about ½ inch oil in a heavy-bottom skillet and heat over medium heat to about 350 degrees. Carefully slide cornmeal patties, one at a time, into hot oil. Do not crowd pan; sides should not touch. Cook until golden and crisp, 3 to 5 minutes. Turn and cook until golden, about 3 minutes longer. Drain on paper towels.

Repeat until all cornbread patties are done, adding additional oil as needed.

Serve with soft butter and honey or warm syrup as a breakfast dish. Serve with cream gravy or alone as a side dish or bread.

¾ CUP CRACKLINGS* OR 4 TO 6 STRIPS THICK BACON (OMIT FOR HOT WATER CORN BREAD)

2 CUPS YELLOW CORNMEAL

1 TEASPOON SALT OR TO TASTE

1 CUP BOILING WATER

2 TABLESPOONS PLUS 1 CUP CORN OR OTHER VEGETABLE OIL FOR FRYING OR AS MUCH AS NEEDED

SOFT BUTTER, HONEY, WARM SYRUP OR CREAM GRAVY (SEE RECIPE ON PAGE 77)

**Cracklings are
small (¼-inch) pieces of pork,
beef or poultry trimmings (fat and skin)
fried until all the fat has been released and
the pieces are brown and crispy. They are
available in some supermarkets, particularly
in the South, or in ethnic markets.
If preparing, fry pieces until golden
and all fat has been rendered.
Drain on paper towels.*

makes 2 dozen

FLAPJACKS

*Call 'em flapjacks, pancakes or griddle cakes,
these griddle-baked rounds of batter are breakfast favorites
around a chuck wagon or ranch kitchen.
The cook could fry up a big batch of bacon and
perform a little short-order magic when a
hungry cowboy got ready for a short or tall stack.
Since flour was a precious commodity, quite likely the
flour would be stretched some with the addition of
some cornmeal. If you make these without the eggs
(as a camp cook might have to), they'll be thin and lacy,
but still delicious.*

1 CUP FLOUR

1 TEASPOON SALT

1 TEASPOON SUGAR

2 TEASPOONS BAKING POWDER

½ TEASPOON BAKING SODA

1¼ CUPS BUTTERMILK OR SOUR MILK

1 EGG, OPTIONAL

¼ CUP MELTED SHORTENING OR
   VEGETABLE OIL

1 TABLESPOON MOLASSES

½ CUP YELLOW CORNMEAL

Preheat a griddle or large, shallow frying pan. In a medium bowl, sift together flour, salt, sugar, baking powder, and baking soda.

In a larger bowl, stir together buttermilk or sour milk, eggs, shortening, or oil and molasses. Add sifted dry ingredients and cornmeal; stir just to moisten ingredients. Don't worry about a few lumps.

To see if griddle is hot enough, splatter a few drops of water on the griddle. If the drops dance and then evaporate, the temperature is right. If too low, the water will puddle and boil; too high, it disappears almost instantly.

Prepare a "test" pancake first. Pour ⅛ to ¼ cup batter onto the griddle. Cook until brown and bubbles break the surface of the uncooked batter side.

Using a spatula, turn and cook until golden on other side. Repeat with remaining batter. Do not allow edges of pancakes to touch when the batter spreads.

makes about 10 large or
14 small flapjacks

BEING A *cowboy* IS ALL I KNOW.

I CAN WORK CATTLE AND COOK

chicken-fried steak.

COWBOYS ARE MEAT-AND-POTATOES PEOPLE.

THERE WEREN'T MANY FRESH VEGETABLES

ON A *chuck wagon.* BUT COWBOYS ALWAYS

HAD GOOD BREADS—*biscuits,* SOURDOUGH.

COWBOYS HAVE ALWAYS BEEN REAL

HIGH ON BISCUITS.

—Grady Spears
Chef of Chisholm Club,
Fort Worth, Texas

CAMP BREAD (BUTTERMILK BISCUITS)

Cowboys often refer to buttermilk biscuits simply as camp bread. No matter what you call them, nothing fortifies like hot biscuits for a long day punching cattle. These tender beauties are worth the practice it takes to get the feel for the dough. Chuck wagon bakers and experienced ranch cooks didn't measure; their sense of touch told them when the proportions were right. Want these to look like they were baked at home on the range? Place them in a lightly greased, black cast-iron skillet.

2 CUPS FLOUR

1 TABLESPOON BAKING POWDER

½ TEASPOON SALT

¼ TEASPOON BAKING SODA

⅓ CUP SHORTENING

¾ CUP BUTTERMILK

Preheat oven to 450°. Have ready an ungreased baking sheet or lightly grease a large (10-inch) black cast-iron skillet.

Stir together flour, baking powder, salt and soda. Cut in shortening using two knives, a pastry cutter, or fingers. Mixture should resemble coarse cornmeal. Make a well in dry ingredients. Pour milk into the well and mix with a fork just until dry ingredients are moistened.

Turn dough out on lightly floured board. Knead lightly 2 or 3 times and pat with fingers or roll out dough about ½-inch thick. If dough is too sticky to handle, knead in just enough flour, a little at a time, until dough holds together.

After rolling, cut with a 2-inch biscuit cutter or flour the rim of a water glass and use as a cutter. Place biscuits on ungreased baking sheet, about 1 inch apart—or place in a lightly greased skillet; sides will touch. Sprinkle lightly with additional flour. Bake 10 to 12 minutes or until golden brown.

makes 10 to 12 biscuits

BOILED COFFEE

4 HEAPING COFFEE MEASURES OF REGULAR OR DECAFFEINATED COARSELY GROUND COFFEE

4 TO 5 CUPS COLD WATER

PINCH SALT

SUGAR, IF DESIRED

SWEETENED CONDENSED MILK OR EVAPORATED MILK

makes 4 cups

Coffee has been as important to cowboys on the range as it has to grunge rockers in Seattle. A chuck wagon that didn't maintain a pot of hot coffee for the cow punchers probably didn't keep a full crew for long. Frankly, boiled coffee can be pretty darn good when what you want is a robust cup of java. Drink it black to stay awake. Add sugar and canned milk or sweetened condensed milk to satisfy a sweet tooth.

In a stovetop coffee pot or saucepan, combine coffee, cold water and salt. Place over high heat and bring water to a boil. As soon as water boils, remove from heat and allow to steep until all the grounds sink to the bottom.

Carefully pour each cup so as to transfer as few grounds as possible. If desired, pour coffee through a filter or strainer.

MAPLE SYRUP SNOW ICE CREAM

1 QUART (4 CUPS) VERY CLEAN SNOW OR SHAVED ICE

½ CUP CONDENSED MILK OR AS NEEDED

¼ CUP MAPLE SYRUP OR TO TASTE

makes 4 servings

Cowboys were known for improvisation in the face of adversity. An early snowfall might make the nights colder but it also meant the creation of ad-libbed ice cream.

Divide snow among four dishes. Pour just enough milk and maple syrup over snow to moisten and create a spoonable consistency. Don't tarry. This stuff disappears fast one way or another.

RANCHING MAY HAVE BEEN ONE OF THE GREAT

BREAKTHROUGHS FOR *women* IN BUSINESS.

WHETHER THEY WERE WIDOWS OR DAUGHTERS

who inherited land,

THEY HAD AN ENTREPRENEURIAL SPIRIT.

MEN HAVE AN EXTRA

appreciation FOR

THE WOMEN WHO CAN *ride* ALONGSIDE.

—Steve Murrin
West Fork Ranch,
Fort Worth, Texas

¼ CUP WATER, BEER, OR APPLE JUICE

1 CUP RAISINS

2½ CUPS FLOUR

1 CUP FRESH BREAD CRUMBS

½ CUP FIRMLY PACKED BROWN SUGAR

1 TEASPOON CINNAMON

¼ TEASPOON GROUND CLOVES

¼ TEASPOON NUTMEG

1 TABLESPOON BAKING SODA

1 TEASPOON SALT

1 CUP GROUND SUET OR
  VEGETABLE SHORTENING

½ CUP CHOPPED PECANS OR WALNUTS

1 5⅓-OUNCE CAN EVAPORATED MILK

½ CUP LIGHT MOLASSES

  WHIPPED CREAM, OPTIONAL

makes 10 to 12 servings

SON-OF-A-GUN-IN-A-SACK

*This is a chuck wagon version of plum pudding.
Without refrigeration, trail drive cooks had to make
do with mostly dry staples, but that didn't eliminate the
cowboys' occasional craving for something sweet.
Hence, this boiled pudding using raisins, nuts, molasses,
and brown sugar. The pudding was shaped like a cannon ball
and placed in a cloth sack, then lowered into a large kettle
of boiling water to cook.*

In a small saucepan, heat water, beer or apple juice to almost boiling. Remove from heat and stir in raisins. Cover and set aside for 5 minutes to soften raisins.

In a large mixing bowl, combine flour, bread crumbs, brown sugar, cinnamon, cloves, nutmeg, baking soda, and salt. Stir in raisins and their liquid, suet or shortening, and nuts, mixing well. Add milk and molasses to make a heavy batter.

Fold 6 to 8 layers of cheesecloth to form a 16-inch square. Use the cheesecloth to line a 1½-quart mixing bowl. Spoon and scrape batter into the lined bowl. Bring up the sides of the cheesecloth, allowing room for the mixture to expand.

Tie ends tightly with string. Bring a large amount of water to a boil over high heat in a Dutch oven or deep kettle. Carefully lower sack into hot water, being careful so that water does not overflow. Ladle out some of the water, if necessary.

Cover, reduce heat, and boil gently for 1½ to 2 hours, or until pudding is firm. Place in a colander to drain and cool for 10 minutes. Unwrap cheesecloth and place pudding, rounded side up, on a plate to cool for 30 minutes before serving. Serve warm with a dollop of whipped cream, if desired.

COOKIE'S SPOON
BATTER COBBLER

*By custom, many chuck wagon cooks were referred to as
"Cookie"—and they were experts at making something
special out of the most meager ingredients.
Canned peaches were a real treat, although fresh peaches
were even better. Make this simplest of simple cobblers
with either one. You can use other fruit, as well—fresh,
frozen or reconstituted dried apples, pears or apricots;
fresh or frozen blueberries, blackberries, strawberries
or a combination.*

Preheat oven to 375°. Grease a shallow 2½-quart casserole or 9x11-inch baking pan. In a large bowl, combine brown sugar, lemon juice and cinnamon, stirring to dissolve sugar. Add peaches (or other fruit) and stir to coat; set aside.

In another large bowl, stir together flour, sugar, baking powder, and salt. Add cream or milk and butter and stir until well-blended. Stir fruit and turn fruit into greased pan. Spoon batter over the fruit and bake for 45 minutes, or until crust is golden. Serve warm or at room temperature, with ice cream or additional cream, if desired.

½ CUP PACKED BROWN SUGAR

1 TABLESPOON LEMON JUICE

¾ TEASPOON GROUND CINNAMON

6 CUPS PEELED AND SLICED PEACHES OR
OTHER FRUIT (IF USING CANNED,
DRAIN THE FRUIT BEFORE MEASURING)

1 CUP FLOUR

¾ CUP SUGAR

2 TEASPOONS BAKING POWDER

¼ TEASPOON SALT

¾ CUP CREAM OR MILK

¼ CUP BUTTER, MELTED

makes 8 servings

I WOULD HATE TO THINK WE'D EVER SELL OUT.

IT HAS TO DO WITH *heritage* AND *family pride.*

OR MAYBE IT'S JUST A GOOD CASE OF *hard-headedness.*

THIS RANCH IS WHO WE ARE.

WE USE ALL THE *resources*

WE HAVE TO KEEP IT GOING.

—*Charles Schreiner IV*
Y.O. Ranch,
Mountain Home, Texas

WILD PLUM
(OR PEACH) "HONEY"

*This isn't made from honey. Rather, it is a syrupy
spread used like jelly or fruit sauce that is easy
to make. And, of course, you can use
farm-raised fruit which, today,
is much easier to find than wild.*

In a medium saucepan over medium heat, combine fruit and sugar, stirring to dissolve sugar. Heat until mixture boils and reduce heat. Stirring frequently, simmer mixture until it thickens to the consistency of honey, about 30 minutes. Stir in vanilla and cinnamon.

Remove from heat and allow to cool. Pour into clean jars, seal, and refrigerate to store. Use as a spread for toast or biscuits, a fruit sauce for pancakes, waffles, French toast, or over ice cream or cake.

2 CUPS COARSELY CHOPPED
   VERY RIPE PLUMS OR PEACHES,
   PEELED AND SEEDED

2 CUPS SUGAR

1 TEASPOON VANILLA

1 TEASPOON CINNAMON, OPTIONAL

makes about
4 (half-pint) jars

RANCH CUISINE

There's nothing like a party on a 1,800-acre spread. Whether that land is the hard-scrabble terrain of the Texas Hill Country, in the shadow of the Colorado Rockies, rolling 'neath the majestic Big Sky, or basking in the Santa Barbara sun, ranch hospitality is unmatched. Whether the fare is grilled beef or wild game, fresh water fish, a pot of chili or buffalo steaks, the party and the food are unforgettable.

Whether the event is a wedding, anniversary, holiday, or just a casual gathering, the event will likely include a variety of meats or fish from nearby pastures, ponds, and woods. A ranch party can transform the simplest food into a feast and a non-occasion into the event of the year.

TEXAS HILL COUNTRY DINNER

The Texas Hill Country, west of San Antonio and Austin, is the heart of the state—the place where the soul of the state resides and where many of the great ranching traditions continue to this day. A typical menu might include beef and wild game, such as quail. In a formal ranch house dining room, where windows may be hung with Irish lace curtains and the table set with silver, crystal and china, cowboy guests outfitted comfortably in well-worn jeans, shiny boots, starched white shirts and Rolex watches, enjoy delectable feasts.

Menu

OYSTER-STUFFED HOT-SMOKED QUAIL
WITH TOMATILLO BUTTER SAUCE

HONEY-ANCHO GLAZED BEEF TENDERLOIN
(OR VENISON BACKSTRAP)

BLACK BEANS WITH CASERA (MEXICAN GOAT CHEESE)

WARM MASHED POTATO SALAD

EL PRESIDENTE SALAD

COWBOY BATTER BREAD

8 WHOLE QUAIL, PREFERABLY WILD
   (WITH OR WITHOUT SKIN)

½ CUP BUTTER, PLUS ADDITIONAL
   AS NEEDED

8 FRESH OYSTERS

1 CUP DRY BREAD CRUMBS

1 TEASPOON SALT OR TO TASTE

1 TEASPOON PEPPER OR TO TASTE

½ TEASPOON CAYENNE PEPPER OR
   TO TASTE (OPTIONAL)

8 STRIPS APPLE-SMOKED BACON

makes 8 appetizer servings;
4 entrees

OYSTER-STUFFED HOT-SMOKED QUAIL

Split quail down the back, rinse and pat dry. Melt butter and allow to cool. Brush quail on all surfaces and refrigerate at least 1 hour, up to 4 hours. Prepare fire for hot smoking. (See page 31.)

Drain oysters and lightly coat all sides with bread crumbs. Place any remaining butter in a small skillet. Add more butter as necessary to coat the bottom of the pan. Heat skillet until butter is warm and bubbly.

Carefully add oysters to skillet, one at a time, and cook until crumbs form a moist crust, about 1 minute. Turn and cook other side, about 1 to 2 minutes longer, until edges begin to curl. Do not cook through. Drain oysters on absorbent towels and reserve.

Generously season buttered quail inside and out with salt and pepper. Lightly sprinkle oysters with cayenne pepper, if desired. The cayenne will give the oysters a spicy bite.

Lay a strip of bacon on a work surface. Place a seasoned quail, meat side down, on the bacon. Snuggle an oyster into the quail cavity and close the breast around the oyster. Wrap the bacon around the breast to hold it closed. Secure bacon with toothpick.

Place quail on preheated smoker, away from direct heat. The internal temperature of the smoker should be about 350°. Cook quail for 30 to 45 minutes or until cooked through. Check several times during smoking, turning several times, as needed for even cooking. Do not overcook or quail will be dry.

Remove quail to a shallow baking pan to catch the juices. Cover with foil to keep warm. Set aside any juices that accumulate and pour over quail just before serving. To serve, carefully remove toothpick, but leave the quail wrapped with bacon. If desired, serve in a puddle of Tomatillo Butter Sauce. (See page 31.)

TOMATILLO BUTTER SAUCE

In a small saucepan, combine white wine and chicken stock. Cook over low heat until liquid is reduced by almost half, to a scant ½ cup. Stir in tomatillo sauce and heat through. Off heat, whisk in softened butter and sherry. Season to taste with salt.

Serve immediately or keep warm at a low temperature. A coffee carafe will hold the sauce at serving temperature for an hour. Do not reheat to boiling or sauce will separate. Serve over grilled poultry, pork, fish, or wild game.

¼ CUP DRY WHITE WINE

½ CUP CHICKEN STOCK

1 8-OUNCE CAN TOMATILLO SAUCE (MEXICAN TOMATILLO SALSA)

2 TABLESPOONS SOFTENED BUTTER

1 TEASPOON SHERRY OR TO TASTE

½ TEASPOON SALT OR TO TASTE

makes about 1½ cups

HOT SMOKING

The technique of hot smoking is somewhere between smoking and grilling. Although similar to smoking, because the food isn't placed directly over the heat source, the temperature inside the cooker is higher—similar to a roasting temperature in an oven—hence, the term "hot smoking."

Several kinds of cookers may be used:

- Grills with separate fireboxes that release smoke and heat into the grill area. These are typically used for barbecuing briskets, ribs, or pork. To achieve a higher cooking temperature, place some hot coals inside the cooker, in the end near the firebox, as well as in the firebox. Place food to be hot smoked near, but not directly over, the coals.
- Grills without a separate fire box require hot coals to one end or to the side of a cooker. Meat should be placed on the grill away from the heat source. With round cookers, start the fire in the middle. Once the coals have burned down to gray ash, push them to the edges, forming an indirect cooking surface in the center of the grill.
- Water smokers are the easiest to use to avoid overcooking. Omit the water pan but put the food to be hot smoked on a grill positioned at the lowest point over the heat source. The fire should be medium.

HONEY-ANCHO GLAZED BEEF TENDERLOIN

(OR VENISON BACKSTRAP)

Remove tenderloin from refrigerator 1 hour before cooking. Rinse and pat dry. Tie ends under or trim to form a neat, even piece of meat. Prepare fire for hot smoking. (See page 31.)

Combine honey and ground chili in a measuring cup. Heat in microwave (or in a small saucepan over low heat) for 10 to 20 seconds, just until thinned and heated through. Stir in oil and allow to cool somewhat.

Season beef with salt and pepper, rubbing spices in. Stir honey mixture and lightly paint all surfaces of beef. Allow to set for 10 minutes. Place tenderloin on preheated smoker, away from direct heat. The internal temperature of the smoker should be about 350°. Cook tenderloin for 30 to 45 minutes or internal temperature reaches 120° for medium rare. Check several times during smoking, turning several times as needed for even cooking. Cover beef loosely and let it rest for 10 to 15 minutes. Slice beef ½- to ¾-inch thick. Serve with accumulated pan juices.

1 4- TO 5-POUND BEEF TENDERLOIN OR
  3 TO 4 VENISON BACKSTRAPS

½ CUP HONEY

1 TABLESPOON FRESH GROUND ANCHO
  CHILI OR CHILI POWDER

¼ CUP VEGETABLE OIL

1 TEASPOON (EACH) SALT AND PEPPER
  OR TO TASTE

makes 8 to 10 servings

2 CUPS DRY BLACK BEANS

½ CUP OLIVE OIL

1 LARGE ONION, FINELY CHOPPED

2 CLOVES GARLIC, CRUSHED

3 QUARTS WATER

2 SMALL TO MEDIUM BAY LEAVES

1 TEASPOON SALT OR TO TASTE

1 TEASPOON PEPPER OR TO TASTE

1 CUP CASERA (MEXICAN GOAT CHEESE)

makes 8 servings

BLACK BEANS
with CASERA

(MEXICAN GOAT CHEESE)

*Prepared like pinto beans, these beautiful black or
turtle beans can make a plate look special.
Their smooth, rich flavor makes them taste delicious.
Rely on a sprinkling of pungent casera
to elevate plain beans.*

Rinse beans and pick them over to remove any debris. Place in a large bowl or stockpot with enough water to cover by several inches. Soak overnight or bring to a boil over high heat. Boil for 1 minute, remove from heat and place a lid on the pan. Allow to sit for 1 hour. After soaking, drain beans and rinse again. In a large saucepan or small stockpot over medium-high heat, combine oil, onions, and garlic. Stir and cook until onions begin to soften, about 3 minutes.

Add beans, 3 quarts water, and bay leaves. Bring liquid to a boil, reduce heat, cover, and simmer until beans are tender—about 4 to 4½ hours. Check the beans every 45 minutes to make sure too much water doesn't cook away. Add additional hot water as needed so water level doesn't drop below beans. Stir occasionally.

When beans soften, remove 1 cup beans and liquid, allow to cool slightly. Place in a blender container and process to the consistency of lumpy mashed potatoes. Return to pot. Remove bay leaves. Add salt and pepper to taste. Cook 30 minutes longer. If softer consistency beans are desired, process additional beans in the blender to desired thickness.

Garnish each serving with a sprinkling of casera.

4 STRIPS OF BACON

3 LARGE RUSSET POTATOES

3 TEASPOONS SALT OR TO TASTE,
DIVIDED USE

¼ CUP MAYONNAISE OR TO TASTE

1 TO 2 TABLESPOONS RESERVED BACON
DRIPPINGS OR TO TASTE

½ CUP SOUR CREAM OR AS NEEDED

½ CUP CHOPPED GREEN ONIONS,
WHITE AND GREEN PARTS

1 TEASPOON BLACK PEPPER OR TO TASTE

1 CUP SHREDDED CHEDDAR CHEESE

¼ CUP FINELY CHOPPED PARSLEY

makes 4 to 6 servings

WARM MASHED POTATO SALAD

*This dish is part mashed potatoes, part potato salad—
a very delicious comfort food.*

Fry bacon until very crisp; set aside drippings. Drain on paper towel. When cool, crumble bacon and reserve. Place potatoes in a large saucepan with enough cold water to cover. Add 2 teaspoons salt and bring water to a boil over high heat. Cook until potatoes are easily pierced with a fork all the way to the middle, about 20 to 30 minutes, depending on the size of the potatoes.

Drain potatoes and cool enough to handle comfortably. Slip off peels and place potatoes in a large bowl or return to large saucepan. Using a potato masher, coarsely mash potatoes. Stir in mayonnaise, bacon drippings to taste, sour cream, green onions, black pepper and additional salt, if needed, to taste.

Heat through over very low heat or transfer potatoes to an oven-safe serving dish and keep warm at 300°.

Just before serving, sprinkle with grated cheese, bacon, and parsley.

COWBOY BATTER BREAD

This is such an easy bread, it's no wonder it was a cowboy favorite. Bake it and present it in a cast-iron skillet for a cowboy look. It also goes well on modern tables as a simple Western focaccia-style bread.

Preheat oven to 425°. Lightly grease a 9- or 10-inch cast-iron skillet (square or round). May also use a square or round baking pan. Sift together flour, baking powder and salt into a medium bowl. Using two knives or a pastry blender, cut in shortening, butter or lard until flour is consistency of large peas. Stir in milk. Dough will be sticky.

To mix with a food processor, combine flour, baking powder and salt in the work bowl. Process briefly using a pulse motion to aerate. Add shortening and milk. Process to form a sticky dough. Spread dough into prepared pan. Bake for 25 to 30 minutes or until dark golden brown. Brush lightly with soft butter. Cut into squares or wedges and serve immediately.

2 CUPS ALL-PURPOSE FLOUR

1 TABLESPOON BAKING POWDER

1 TEASPOON SALT

6 TABLESPOONS VEGETABLE SHORTENING, BUTTER, OR LARD (OR A COMBINATION FOR FLAVOR)

1¼ CUPS MILK

Western focaccia:
To present bread in this way, brush with garlic-flavored olive oil upon removing bread from oven. Sprinkle lightly with grated Parmesan cheese. Return to oven briefly, just to melt cheese.

3 TO 4 FIRM CUCUMBERS

1 LARGE SWEET ONION
(PREFERABLY A TEXAS 1015)

⅞ CUP WHITE VINEGAR

⅛ CUP WATER

¼ CUP SUGAR

1 TEASPOON SALT

½ TEASPOON BLACK PEPPER

2 VINE-RIPE TOMATOES

2 RIPE AVOCADOS

½ CUP COARSELY CHOPPED FRESH MINT

EL PRESIDENTE SALAD

*This is a variation on the cucumber salad known as
LBJ salad, a favorite of the late president
Lyndon B. Johnson, who served it frequently on his
Texas Hill Country ranch.*

Strip-peel cucumbers by cutting off ends, then peeling strips, leaving some stripes of green peel. Cut cucumber in half, then into quarters, lengthwise. Cut cucumbers into ½-inch pieces. Place in nonreactive bowl.

Coarsely chop onion and toss with cucumber. Combine vinegar, water, sugar, salt, and pepper in a jar or container with tight lid. Shake until sugar is dissolved. Taste and adjust seasoning as desired. Dressing should be sweet-and-sour but not too sweet. Adjust seasoning with a pinch of salt before adding more sugar.

Refrigerate at least an hour or as long as overnight. Just before serving, coarsely chop tomatoes and allow to drain. Meanwhile, peel and coarsely chop avocados. Add drained tomatoes, avocados, and mint to salad, tossing to coat all ingredients.

OUR *ranch* IS A WAY TO CONNECT

THE *generations.*

ALTHOUGH WE ALL LIVE FAIRLY CLOSE

TOGETHER IN HOUSTON,

WHEN WE ALL GO UP THERE—

JOHN AND I, THE *children* AND

grandchildren — WE SEE EACH OTHER

IN A DIFFERENT WAY.

—Elizabeth Ann (Bitsy) Hill
wife of former Texas Supreme Court Justice and State Attorney General,
John Hill,
Houston, Texas

NEW MEXICO
RED AND GREEN
CHILE RANCH BUFFET

*A log cookhouse, at a modern dude ranch or
on a working ranch in the mountains, could be the setting for
a casual lunch or supper featuring hearty chile stews.
Even though the days are warm,
mornings and evenings are cool.
Whether the day's activity involved skiing, a trail ride,
or working cattle, a bowl or two of chile stew—green and
red—will fortify a cowboy. Fresh corn and flour tortillas are
the best way to soak up the juices.
Finish the meal with a taste of summer—easy
peach honey preserves—and hot Indian fry bread.*

Menu

NEW MEXICO GREEN CHILE STEW

CHILI COLORADO

POSOLE

FLOUR TORTILLAS

CORN TORTILLAS

INDIAN FRY BREAD WITH PEACH HONEY (RECIPE PG. 27)

NEW MEXICO GREEN CHILE STEW

*This is the stuff that has made New Mexico famous—
those pungent, fresh-roasted green chilies combined with . . .
well, they're good with just about anything, from eggs to cheese.
They are especially good with beef or pork.*

Cut meat into ½-inch cubes or use coarse ground beef for chili. Heat oil in a Dutch oven or stew pot over medium heat. Add meat and cook until meat begins to brown. Stir in onions and cook until onions begin to soften. Add water and bring liquid to a boil. Reduce heat, cover and simmer until meat is tender, about 1 hour.

Stir in green chilies, tomatoes, cumin, leaf oregano, and garlic. Cover and simmer until mixture forms a thick stew, about 30 to 35 minutes. To thicken, remove lid and cook until some of the liquid cooks away. Serve in bowls with warm flour or corn tortillas, purchased or homemade.

**To roast green chilies, preheat
oven broiler. Place in single layer on shallow pan.
Place about 6 inches under heat and cook, turning frequently,
until skins are blistered and charred in spots. Place chilies in a
plastic bag, seal and allow to steam for 20 minutes. Remove from
bag and allow to cool enough to handle. Peel away skin under
running water. Pat chilies dry and use as recipe directs.
To store unused roasted chilies, cover with oil
and refrigerate up to 2 weeks.*

1½ POUNDS LEAN PORK (OR BEEF) FOR STEW

1 TABLESPOON VEGETABLE OIL

1 CUP CHOPPED ONION

1 CUP HOT WATER

3 4-OUNCE CANS CHOPPED GREEN CHILIES OR 8 FRESH ROASTED AND PEELED CHILIES, CHOPPED*

1 8-OUNCE CAN CHOPPED TOMATOES AND LIQUID (OR CHOP WHOLE CANNED TOMATOES, RESERVING LIQUID) OR 3 TO 4 MEDIUM FRESH TOMATOES, CHOPPED

1 TEASPOON CUMIN

½ TEASPOON LEAF OREGANO

2 CLOVES GARLIC, FINELY CHOPPED

WARM FLOUR (SEE PAGE 45) OR CORN TORTILLAS (SEE PAGE 47)

makes 6 to 8 servings

CHILE COLORADO

Chile Colorado is a red chile stew using pork that is popular in West Texas and New Mexico. Hispanic ranchhands often have a deft touch with this fiery concoction. It should be cooked the day before serving. Refrigerate overnight and lift away congealed fat; discard.

Neckbones in the pot are optional, but they add special flavoring and are great for gnawing if you want a real ranchhand experience. Don't confuse this with chili con carne. They're different dishes with different flavor profiles.

Trim external fat from pork; set aside. Place pork in Dutch oven or stewpot. Add enough water to cover. Bring liquid to a boil, reduce heat to simmer, cover and cook for 1½ hours or until pork is very tender.

Remove the meat (shoulder and neck bones); reserving cooking liquid. Allow shoulder to cool enough to handle. Cut meat away from the bone and chop into ½-inch cubes. Store cubed pork and neck bones, if using, in refrigerator overnight. Place cooking liquid in a large (separate) sealed container and refrigerate overnight or several hours until fat hardens. Lift fat from surface and discard.

4 POUNDS PORK SHOULDER
(ALSO KNOWN AS PORK BUTT)

3 TO 4 POUNDS PORK NECK BONE
(OPTIONAL)

3 TO 3½ QUARTS WATER

½ CUP CORNMEAL OR MASA, HARINA

½ CUP COLD WATER

½ TO ¾ CUP, OR TO TASTE GROUND NEW
MEXICO RED CHILE (PURCHASED OR
FRESHLY GROUND*)

2 CLOVES GARLIC

1½ TEASPOONS SALT OR TO TASTE
(DIVIDED USE)

1½ TEASPOONS LEAF OREGANO OR
TO TASTE (DIVIDED USE)

½ CUP HOT WATER

JUICE FROM ½ LEMON OR LIME,
OR TO TASTE

GARNISHES: FINELY CHOPPED OR
GROUND WHITE ONION, FINELY
CHOPPED CILANTRO AND LIME OR
LEMON WEDGES

WARM FLOUR (SEE PAGE 45) OR
CORN TORTILLAS (SEE PAGE 47)

*To grind dried New Mexico red chilies:
Remove stems from 12 dried New Mexico red chilies. Shake out seeds. Heat a heavy-bottom skillet over medium-high heat. In dry skillet, heat chilies until lightly toasted on all sides. Turn frequently and watch carefully to avoid burning. Place chilies a few at a time in blender container and process until finely chopped or even longer for a finer texture.

makes 10 servings

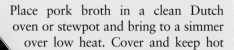

Place pork broth in a clean Dutch oven or stewpot and bring to a simmer over low heat. Cover and keep hot but do not allow liquid to boil and reduce. Meanwhile, combine New Mexico red chile powder, 2 cloves garlic, ½ teaspoon salt, ½ teaspoon leaf oregano, and hot water in blender container. Process to make a loose, pourable puree; set aside.

In a heavy-bottom skillet, heat reserved pieces of pork fat over medium heat to render about 2 tablespoons fat or use 2 tablespoons vegetable oil. Remove remaining pieces of solid fat and discard. Turn up heat. When fat or oil smokes, add pork cubes in several batches. Stir and cook until cubes are brown and crispy. Add browned pork, along with neck bones (if using), to the broth.

Pour about ½ cup broth into the skillet to deglaze. Stir to loosen any bits of meat stuck to the bottom of the skillet. In a small bowl, stir together cornmeal or masa, 1 teaspoon salt, 1 teaspoon leaf oregano and water to make a smooth paste. Gradually add mixture to skillet, stirring to avoid lumps. Simmer until thickened, about 5 minutes.

Pour thickened broth into the pot and stir in red chile mixture. Simmer for 25 minutes; mixture should be slightly thickened but soupy. Add water if needed and cook 15 minutes longer. Adjust seasoning with salt, oregano, and a squeeze of fresh lemon or lime.

Serve with additional finely chopped or grated fresh white onion, finely chopped cilantro and plenty of lime or lemon wedges. Serve also with plenty of warm flour tortillas. Neck bones can be served in bowls with the chili. They're fun to gnaw on, if the meat hasn't all cooked off. Serve with warm flour or corn tortillas.

1 TABLESPOON VEGETABLE OIL OR
RENDERED PORK FAT

1 LARGE ONION, CHOPPED

2 POUNDS BONELESS CHICKEN BREAST
OR PORK SHOULDER (ALSO KNOWN AS
PORK BUTT), CUT INTO 1-INCH CUBES

2 CLOVES GARLIC, FINELY CHOPPED

2 QUARTS CHICKEN BROTH

1 BAY LEAF

2 TEASPOONS LEAF OREGANO

4 TABLESPOONS GROUND NEW MEXICO
RED CHILE OR ½ CUP CHOPPED,
ROASTED GREEN CHILIES, OR TO TASTE

2 TEASPOONS SALT OR TO TASTE

2 CUPS CANNED HOMINY, DRAINED
(IF USING DRIED POSOLE,
RECONSTITUTE ACCORDING TO
PACKAGE DIRECTIONS TO MAKE 2 CUPS)

SHREDDED MILD CHEDDAR OR
MONTEREY JACK CHEESE FOR GARNISH

WARM FLOUR (SEE PAGE 45) OR
CORN TORTILLAS (SEE PAGE 47)

makes 8 servings

POSOLE

Posole is better known in some parts of the country as hominy. For those who aren't familiar with either, posole (or hominy) consists of white or yellow corn kernels from which the hull and germs have been removed by soaking in slaked lime or lye. It can be purchased dried (and needing reconstituting) or canned (already reconstituted). It is the signature ingredient in New Mexican stews, with a broth often flavored and colored by red or green chilies. These stews are also called posole. This version uses chicken or pork.

Heat oil or render fat trimmed from pork shoulder in a Dutch oven or large stewpot over medium heat. Add onion and cook until onions begin to soften. Add pork, stirring and cooking until pork is nicely browned.

Stir in garlic and cook just until garlic is fragrant. Add chicken broth, bay leaf, oregano, and ground red chile or roasted green chile. Simmer about 1 hour or until pork is tender. Stir in posole.

Adjust seasoning to taste. Cook about 20 minutes longer.

Serve in bowls with warm flour or corn tortillas. Garnish generously with cheese, if desired.

Shortcut: Use 1½ quarts chicken broth and 2 8-ounce cans enchilada sauce to simmer the browned pork. Eliminate bay leaf, oregano, and red chili. Simmer 1 hour or until pork is tender. Check to make sure liquid does not evaporate during cooking. Add salt to taste.

FLOUR TORTILLAS

Making flour tortillas will give you a new appreciation for purchased ones. Homemade are always better when you get the technique down. Excellent flour tortillas are available, however, in supermarkets, restaurants, Hispanic markets, and bakeries.

In a large bowl, mix together flour and baking powder. Using fingers, a pastry cutter, or two knives, work the shortening or lard into the flour to form a crumbly mixture.

Heat water to lukewarm (100° to 120°) and dissolve salt in it. Add water to flour, stirring to blend well and form a dough. Knead in the bowl for 2 to 3 minutes, until no longer sticky. Cover loosely with a kitchen towel and let rest for 30 minutes, up to 2 hours.

Knead dough briefly, then form balls about 1½ inches in diameter. On a lightly floured board, roll out the balls into circles as thin as possible, at least 6 to 8 inches in diameter.

Preheat a heavy griddle, preferably cast iron. When hot, place tortillas on ungreased griddle and cook until lightly browned, about 30 seconds. Turn and cook on the other side, until tortilla puffs slightly and edges brown. If a tortilla puffs too much, gently press it down with a spatula.

Keep warm by covering with a clean towel. Tortillas may be reheated on the griddle or by wrapping in paper towels and microwaving for about 1 to 2 minutes (30 seconds at a time) for a dozen tortillas. Larger batches may be wrapped in foil and heated in a 300° oven for 20 minutes.

2½ CUPS FLOUR

2½ TEASPOONS BAKING POWDER

1½ TEASPOONS SALT

¾ CUP LARD OR SHORTENING

1 CUP WARM WATER

Tip: Use measured stick shortening—1¼ sticks for this recipe—for a fluffier, easier to work dough.

makes about 2 dozen

CORN TORTILLAS

*Using masa harina, a prepared mix for corn tortillas,
simplifies the process of making corn tortillas. It is much easier
than starting with dried corn kernels and ground limestone.
A tortilla press, a simple gadget resembling an old-fashioned
waffle iron, makes it easier to make rounds of uniform
shape and thickness. Whether you make them, or find a
restaurant or bakery that makes them, nothing beats
a fresh, warm corn tortilla.*

2 CUPS MASA HARINA

1 CUP WATER

In a small bowl, combine masa harina and water and mix until dough forms a ball. If mixture seems dry, add water 1 tablespoon at a time until dough holds together. Shape dough into 1½-inch balls. Return to bowl and cover with a damp cloth. Place ball between two sheets of plastic wrap or two plastic bags. You can also use wax paper.

Preheat a heavy griddle or skillet.

Roll dough into 6-inch circles using a rolling pin or place between plates of tortilla press and apply even pressure to form the masa disks. Carefully peel off layers of plastic or wax paper and place tortilla on ungreased griddle or in dry skillet and cook for about 1 minute or until lightly browned at edges. Turn and cook another 15 to 20 seconds or until tortilla is lightly browned and begins to puff.

Keep warm by covering with a clean towel. Tortillas may be reheated on the griddle or by wrapping in paper towels and microwaving for 1 to 2 minutes for a dozen tortillas. Larger batches may be wrapped in foil and heated in a 300° oven for 20 minutes.

makes 16 to 18 tortillas

2 CUPS UNBLEACHED FLOUR

½ TEASPOON BAKING SODA

½ TEASPOON SALT

¼ CUP SHORTENING

¾ CUP BEER OR WATER

2 CUPS VEGETABLE COOKING OIL

*Cinnamon sugar:
Combine 1 to 2 teaspoons cinnamon with 1 cup sugar. Mix well to evenly distribute cinnamon.

makes about 2 dozen small pieces, about 1 dozen large

INDIAN FRY BREAD

This is a dessert similar to sopaipillas. The dough is somewhat coarser but still fragrant and tender. For an after-dinner sweet, sprinkle fry breads with cinnamon sugar as soon as they come out of the fryer. For a bread to fill with chili, shredded meat, or barbecue, omit the cinnamon sugar.

Sift together flour, baking soda, and salt into a medium bowl. Using two knives or a pastry blender, cut in shortening until flour is consistency of large peas. Make a well in the center of the dough and add beer or water all at once.

Stir just until the mixture forms a ball.

To mix with a food processor, combine flour and baking soda in the work bowl. Process briefly using a pulse motion to aerate. Add shortening and process until flour is consistency of large peas. Add beer or water and process just until dough forms a ball. Knead gently, 10 to 12 times, on a lightly floured surface.

To mix with an electric mixer, attach dough hook and combine flour and baking soda in mixer bowl. Process to combine dry ingredients. Add shortening and process until flour is consistency of large peas. Add beer or water and process until dough is smooth and handles relatively easily. Omit kneading step.

Pinch off about 1 tablespoon of dough and roll into a ball. Using a rolling pin (or your hands), shape the dough into a thin round, about 3 inches in diameter.

Heat oil to 380°. To test frying temperature, pinch off a small piece of dough and drop into hot oil. The dough should blister and puff instantly if oil is hot enough.

Alternate shaping method: Roll out dough on floured surface to a ½-inch thickness. Cut into 4- or 5-inch squares or 8-inch disks. Carefully slide pieces of dough, one at a time, into hot oil. Do not crowd. Quickly baste top of dough with hot oil so surfaces fry evenly. Turn if needed. Total cooking time is about 2 minutes or until bread is golden on all sides. Drain on paper towels.

Wait a minute between batches to allow oil to return to correct frying temperature.

Fry breads can be eaten with savory dishes, such as chili, or filled with shredded meat, chicken, pork, or barbecue. As a dessert, sprinkle fry breads with cinnamon sugar* while hot. Serve immediately with Peach Honey, syrup, jelly, or real honey.

BIG SKY
WILD GAME FEAST

*Open spaces, rolling hills and shimmering lakes reflecting
snow-capped mountains in Wyoming, Montana, Nebraska,
North and South Dakota set dramatic backdrops for ranch life.
Because spaces are vast, ranchers traditionally kept houses in
town—many of which are lovely Victorians.*

*Whether this menu is enjoyed on a ranch or in town,
it portrays some of the best the land and water have to offer.*

Menu

MOUNTAIN LAKE DUCK PÂTÉ
WITH DRIED CHERRY CHUTNEY
AND HOT WATER CORNBREAD

GRILLED SALMON TROUT

BRAISED PHEASANT WITH PINE NUTS

SALISBURY BUFFALO STEAK BURGERS
WITH GREEN CHILE MAYONNAISE
AND AVOCADO SALSA CRUDA

GINGER PEAR STACK CAKE

1 POUND SKINLESS DUCK BREAST OR
  SKINLESS DUCK BREAST PLUS MEAT
  CUT FROM FROM LEG QUARTERS

¼ POUND BULK PORK SAUSAGE

1 LARGE SHALLOT, FINELY CHOPPED

½ CUP BUTTER

3 TABLESPOONS DRY SHERRY

½ TEASPOON SALT OR TO TASTE

½ TEASPOON BLACK PEPPER

1 TEASPOON JUNIPER BERRIES, CRUSHED

1 TO 2 TEASPOONS LEMON JUICE,
  OPTIONAL

HOT WATER CORNBREAD
(SEE PAGE 17)

DRIED CHERRY CHUTNEY

makes 16 servings

*For a Southern and
Western twist, serve with small
ovals of Hot Water Corn Bread,
and bottled pickled okra.*

MOUNTAIN LAKE DUCK PÂTÉ

*Wild or domestic duck makes a delicious and earthy pâté.
Set it off with Dried Cherry Chutney.*

Cut duck pieces into 2-inch pieces; set aside. Over medium heat, crumble pork sausage into a large skillet over low heat. Stir to break sausage into very small pieces. Cook until pork is no longer pink, 3 to 4 minutes.

Add duck pieces, stirring and cooking over low heat until duck is cooked through, about 10 minutes. Add shallots, lower heat, stir and cook just until shallots are soft. Do not allow ingredients to crisp.

Place duck-sausage mixture in blender. Allow to cool slightly. Melt butter in same skillet. Add sherry and remove from heat. Pour into blender. Add salt, pepper, and crushed juniper berries. Process to form a fine-grained spread.

To create an even texture, stop blender and scrape down ingredients several times. Taste and adjust seasonings, adding lemon juice to taste, if desired. Pack mixture into a loaf pan or 2-cup mold. Smooth top. Cover tightly with plastic wrap and refrigerate to chill completely, preferably overnight. Serve slighty chilled or at room temperature with water crackers, toast, cornichons, spicy mustard, and Dried Cherry Chutney.

DRIED CHERRY CHUTNEY

*This simple chutney is a beautiful accent to the duck pâté.
It could also substitute for cranberry sauce at Thanksgiving
or as a garnish for almost any wild game, pork, or roast fowl.*

Place cherries in nonreactive bowl and cover with boiling water. Let stand for 30 minutes. Drain cherries and reserve. Place soaking liquid in a small saucepan over medium heat. Reduce to about 2 tablespoons liquid.

To reduced soaking liquid, add cherries, brown sugar, onion slices, ginger, cider vinegar and salt. Bring to a boil, then reduce heat to very low temperature. Simmer about 30 minutes, stirring occasionally. Let cool completely. Refrigerate until ready to serve.

6 OUNCES DRIED CHERRIES

¾ CUP BOILING WATER

½ CUP PACKED LIGHT BROWN SUGAR

1 SMALL ONION, THINLY SLICED

½ TEASPOON GROUND GINGER

½ CUP CIDER VINEGAR

¼ TEASPOON SALT

makes about 1 1/2 cups

GRILLED SALMON TROUT

4 2-POUND SALMON TROUT

4 TABLESPOONS DIJON MUSTARD

½ CUP (1 STICK) BUTTER

1 CLOVE GARLIC, FINELY CHOPPED

4 TABLESPONS BROWN SUGAR

½ CUP APPLE CIDER OR WHITE WINE

1 TEASPOON WORCESTERSHIRE SAUCE

2 TEASPOONS TOMATO SAUCE OR KETCHUP

Lake and river trout are a delicacy and they would be wonderful in this recipe. For home consumption, however, consider salmon trout, a hybrid that is bigger than a trout and smaller than most salmon. Because of their size, they're easier to cook than larger, whole fish. Farm-raised, they are widely available. Wild or farm-raised salmon or trout may also be prepared this way. A flat grill basket makes it easier to get the fish on and off the grill without falling apart. Adjust cooking time for the size of the fish.

Prepare coals for a medium to medium-hot fire. Rinse and dry trout. Set aside. In a small saucepan, combine mustard, butter, garlic, brown sugar, apple cider or wine, Worcestershire sauce and tomato sauce over low heat. Melt, stirring constantly, until sugar dissolves. Do not allow butter to separate. The sauce should be thick.

Spray grill basket with cooking spray or—off heat—spray the grill. Open fish flat on grill basket. Baste both sides with sauce. When coals are hot and covered with gray ash, place cooker with salmon, flesh side down, on grill.

Total cooking time should be about 10 minutes per inch of thickness at thickest part. Depending on thickness, cook about 7 to 8 minutes on flesh side, turn and cook skin-side down for 3 to 4 minutes.

makes 8 servings

BRAISED PHEASANT
with PINE NUTS

*Besides duck and trout, the northern Plains
are known for their upland game birds.
Few wild fowl are as elegant
and delicious as pheasant.*

Preheat oven to 325°. Season pheasant on all sides with salt and pepper. In a large skillet over medium heat, combine butter and cooking oil. Cook pheasant on all sides until brown. Remove pheasant to a shallow baking dish. Arrange in a single layer.

In the same skillet, cook the onions until wilted and golden at the edges. Pour wine into skillet. Remove from heat and stir to loosen any bits stuck to the bottom. Pour onions and wine around pheasant. Cover tightly with foil and place in oven for 45 minutes to 1 hour, depending upon size. Remove foil, baste and bake 15 minutes longer. Remove birds and onion to serving platter; cover and keep warm.

Measure 1 cup cooking liquid from roasting pan and pour into skillet over low heat. Stir in cream, thyme, ¼ teaspoon salt and ⅛ teaspoon pepper. Simmer, stirring frequently, over low heat about 5 minutes or until flavors blend and sauce thickens slightly.

Slice breast meat from bone. Separate legs and thighs into serving pieces. Serve sliced pheasant and leg pieces topped with a mound of onion in a puddle of sauce, with additional sauce drizzled on top. Sprinkle with toasted pine nuts.

2 SMALL 2-POUND WILD PHEASANTS, OR
  1 LARGE (3½–4 POUND) FARM-RAISED
  PHEASANT, HALVED

1¼ TEASPOONS SALT OR TO TASTE,
  DIVIDED USE

1⅛ TEASPOONS PEPPER OR TO TASTE,
  DIVIDED USE

1 TABLESPOON BUTTER

1 TABLESPOON VEGETABLE COOKING OIL

1 LARGE SWEET ONION,
  CUT INTO THIN RINGS

1 CUP DRY WHITE OR RED WINE

¾ CUP CREAM

2 TEASPOONS FRESH THYME LEAVES

½ CUP TOASTED PINE NUTS

makes 4 servings

2 POUNDS GROUND BUFFALO
(MAY USE BEEF, VENISON, OR ELK)

¾ CUP FINELY CRUSHED ICE (OPTIONAL)

2 TABLESPOONS WORCESTERSHIRE
SAUCE

1½ TEASPOONS STEAK SEASONING BLEND
OR SALT TO TASTE

1 TEASPOON BLACK PEPPER OR TO TASTE

1 CUP BOTTLED BARBECUE SAUCE OR
HOMEMADE BARBECUE SAUCE

4 ENGLISH MUFFIN HALVES OR
4 HAMBURGER BUNS

SOFT BUTTER

GREEN CHILI MAYONNAISE

AVOCADO SALSA CRUDA

makes 4 servings

SALISBURY BUFFALO STEAK BURGERS

with

GREEN CHILE MAYONNAISE

and

AVOCADO SALSA CRUDA

Buffalos don't roam the plains by the thousands any more, but farm-raised buffalo is still a popular—and relatively low-fat— red meat. Adding crushed ice to a ground meat patty helps the meat stay moist and juicy over the coals or on the griddle.

Prepare fire for medium coals. If desired, burgers may be cooked on a griddle or in a skillet over medium-high heat. As coals begin to glow orange and turn gray with ash, place meat in a large bowl. Combine meat, crushed ice, Worcestershire sauce, seasoning blend, and pepper. Working quickly, stir or knead in ingredients to evenly distribute ice and seasonings.

Divide meat into 4 portions of equal size. Shape each into a ball, then flatten to a thickness of about 1 inch. When coals are covered with gray ash, grill burgers to desired degree of doneness, about 6–8 minutes. If using buffalo, be particularly careful not to place over too hot coals or overcook since the meat contains very little fat and is prone to drying. Cook to medium done.

About 1 to 2 minutes before burgers are done, brush one side lightly with barbecue sauce. Turn and brush the other side. Cook a minute or two, then turn once more to glaze before removing from fire.

1 4-OUNCE CAN GREEN CHILIES OR
   ¼ CUP FRESH ROASTED GREEN CHILIES

1½ CUPS MAYONNAISE,
   HOMEMADE OR BOTTLED

makes 1¹/₂ cups

2 LARGE, RIPE TOMATOES (ABOUT 2 CUPS
   COARSELY CHOPPED)

1 TO 2 TABLESPOONS FINELY CHOPPED
   FRESH JALAPEÑO PEPPERS OR
   TO TASTE

¼ CUP ONION, FINELY CHOPPED

1 CLOVE GARLIC, FINELY CHOPPED

½ TEASPOON SALT OR TO TASTE

1 SMALL, RIPE AVOCADO

1 TO 2 TEASPOONS LEMON JUICE OR
   TO TASTE

makes about 1¹/₂ cups

If preparing on a griddle or in a skillet, cook about 10 minutes, brushing each side with barbecue sauce during final minutes of cooking. Keep warm.

Spread cut side of English muffin halves or hamburger buns with soft butter and grill or toast until butter melts. Spread cut side generously with Green Chile Mayonnaise. Serve buffalo burgers open-faced on English muffin half or between halves of buns. Garnish with a dollop of Avocado Salsa Cruda.

GREEN CHILE MAYONNAISE

Drain green chilies, if using canned. Place chilies in blender or food processor and process until smooth. Add mayonnaise and process just until combined.

AVOCADO SALSA CRUDA

(FRESH SALSA WITH AVOCADO)

Combine tomatoes, peppers, onion and garlic in a medium bowl. Toss to combine. Add salt, mixing well. Allow to stand about 1 hour.

Peel, seed and coarsely chop avocado. Add to salsa. Adjust seasoning with salt and lemon juice.

GINGER PEAR STACK CAKE

This was a traditional wedding cake in mountain pioneer and cowboy weddings—that is, when you could get a cowboy to settle down. Guests brought a layer of cake and cooked fruit was then spread between layers. This version, however, doesn't rely on the kindness of neighbors. You can make homemade gingerbread or buy a storebought cake and split the layers.

Peel and core pears (or apples). Cut fruit into quarters. Place fruit in a medium saucepan or skillet with high sides. Add water to almost cover, brandy, and sugar. Bring liquid to a boil, reduce heat, cover and simmer until fruit is soft, about 10 minutes.

Remove from heat. Using a potato masher, coarsely mash the fruit. If pear sauce is too soupy, return to low heat and simmer until liquid is reduced to the consistency of thick applesauce. Add lemon juice as needed for flavor. Fruit should be chunky. Set aside and cool, then refrigerate and chill completely.

Preheat oven to 375°. Grease and flour 3 round 8 x 1½-inch baking pans.

In a large mixing bowl, beat together butter and sugar until light and fluffy. Beat in molasses. Then add eggs, one at a time, beating well after each addition.

In a separate bowl, stir together flour, ginger, baking soda and salt; add to cream mixture alternately with beer, beating well after each addition.

Pour 1⅓ cups batter into each prepared pan. Reserve remaining batter in refrigerator. Bake about 15 minutes or until cake tests done—a toothpick inserted in the center should come out clean.

Cool in pans about 5 minutes, then turn layers out onto wire racks to cool completely.

Wash pans and grease and flour a second time. Fill pans with batter as before and bake according to above directions. Cool and turn out on racks to cool.

To assemble cake, place one layer, bottom-side up, on a cake plate. Spread chilled pear sauce over cake. Repeat, layering cake and pear sauce, ending with a layer of cake. Chill if not serving right away.

Just before serving, beat cream in a chilled bowl using chilled electric beaters. Beat cream until soft peaks form. Spread whipped cream on top; garnish with fresh sliced pears.

2½ POUNDS PEARS (OR APPLES)

1 CUP WATER OR AS NEEDED

1 TABLESPOON BRANDY OR BOURBON, OPTIONAL

½ CUP SUGAR OR TO TASTE

1 TEASPOON LEMON JUICE OR TO TASTE

1 CUP BUTTER

1 CUP SUGAR

1 CUP LIGHT MOLASSES

3 EGGS

4 CUPS FLOUR

1 TABLESPOON GROUND GINGER

1 TEASPOON BAKING SODA

1 TEASPOON SALT

1 CUP LAGER OR DARK BEER

1 CUP CREAM, WELL-CHILLED

SLICED FRESH PEARS FOR GARNISH

makes 10 to 12 servings

RANCHO
SMOKED SIRLOIN

*California cowboys in the Santa Maria Valley have a particular
way with beef and a style of hot-smoking based on Spanish
ranch tradition. In its purest form, Santa Maria barbecue
requires a hard-to-find (outside California) cut called tri-tip
roast and red oak wood for the fire.*

*This tradition grew out of grilled lunches prepared for
mostly Hispanic farm and ranch workers using a tough,
less desirable cut of beef. In today's California,
Santa Maria-style barbecue is a special way of entertaining.*

*The menu includes chunky tomato salsa, beans, macaroni and
cheese. The following recipes have been adapted to make the
style of cooking more accessible. Sirloin has been substituted for
tri-tip. More widely available pintos substitute for the smaller,
regional favorite called pinquinto beans.*

*Nevertheless, the flavors, casual style and California emphasis
on use of fresh ingredients for the salsa make this a meal
vaqueros would recognize—and love.*

*With considerable adaptation, the following beef receipe is from
the Santa Maria Chamber of Commerce.*

Menu

RANCHO SMOKED SIRLOIN

VALLEY SALSA

RANCH PEPPER BREAD

VAQUERO BEANS
MACARONI AND CHEESE (SEE PAGE 71)

FLAN

RANCHO SMOKED SIRLOIN

This recipe uses a technique called "hot-smoking." The meat is cooked at higher temperatures then traditional barbecue to produce beautiful medium rare slices that are juicy and tender. See page 31.

Prepare fire for medium hot coals, about 350 F to 375 F. An hour before cooking, remove meat from refrigerator. Generously season on all sides with garlic salt and pepper.

Place meat directly over hot coals and sear on all sides to brown, about 10 minutes. Place lid on cooker while meat browns but check frequently to prevent charring.

When meat is brown move to a cooler portion of the grill, ideally 300 F to 325 F. Turn and cook as needed to produce a medium (warm, red) center, about 45 minutes cooking time.

Remove meat from grill and allow to rest 15 minutes, loosely tented with foil. Slice thin, setting aside any juices that accumulate, and serve immediately. Pour juices over meat just before serving. Serve with Valley Salsa.

1 2-INCH THICK SIRLOIN STEAK (3 TO 4 POUNDS)

1 TEASPOON (EACH) GARLIC SALT AND PEPPER, OR TO TASTE

VALLEY SALSA

makes 8 to 10 servings

VALLEY SALSA

This is a cross between a typical Mexican salsa and a Spanish gazpacho.

In a nonreactive bowl, combine tomatoes, celery, onions, green chilies, cilantro, vinegar, Worcestershire sauce, and salt. Cover and let stand for 1 hour so flavors blend. Stir in oil just before serving.

3 MEDIUM TOMATOES, COARSELY CHOPPED

½ CUP SLICED CELERY

½ CUP SLICED GREEN ONIONS, WHITE AND GREEN PARTS

½ CUP SLICED FRESH CALIFORNIA (ANAHEIM) GREEN CHILIES

2 TABLESPOONS CHOPPED FRESH CILANTRO LEAVES

2 CLOVES GARLIC, FINELY CHOPPED

1 TABLESPOON WHITE VINEGAR

DASH WORCESTERSHIRE SAUCE

½ TEASPOON SALT OR TO TASTE

¼ CUP EXTRA VIRGIN OLIVE OIL, OR TO TASTE

makes 3½ cups

1 LARGE LOAF OF FRENCH BREAD

½ CUP SOFTENED BUTTER OR AS NEEDED

2 TABLESPOONS COARSELY CRACKED
BLACK PEPPER OR AS NEEDED

makes 6 to 8 servings

1 POUND DRY PINTO (OR NAVY) BEANS

1 TABLESPOON OLIVE OIL

½ CUP CHOPPED HAM OR SPANISH
CHORIZO (DRY SAUSAGE)

1 CLOVE GARLIC, FINELY CHOPPED

1 (8-OUNCE) CAN TOMATO SAUCE

¼ CUP CHILI SAUCE

1 TABLESPOON SUGAR

1 TEASPOON YELLOW MUSTARD

1 TEASPOON SALT OR TO TASTE

makes 8 to 10 servings

RANCH PEPPER BREAD

Hot bread is a must with juicy red meat.

Cut bread into 1-inch thick slices. Reconstruct the loaf in a double thickness of foil. Spread butter between each slice and season each slice to taste with a sprinkle of black pepper.

Wrap the bread tightly in foil. Place on a relatively cool part of the grill during the last 10 minutes of cooking or heat at 300° for 10 minutes in the oven. Keep warm until serving time.

VAQUERO BEANS

These beans would work great with any barbecue—beef, pork or chicken. Navy beans may be substituted, if desired.

Rinse beans and remove any small stones or shriveled beans. Place in a large bowl or saucepan, add enough water to cover and soak overnight. After soaking, drain, place in large saucepan and add enough water to cover. Over high heat, bring beans to a boil, reduce heat, cover and simmer 2 to 3 hours, or until tender.

Meanwhile, place olive oil, ham and garlic in a small saucepan over medium heat. Cook 2 to 3 minutes, stirring frequently. Add tomato sauce, chili sauce, sugar, and mustard. Stir and remove from heat, set aside.

Drain cooking liquid from beans and reserve. Pour sauce over beans, stirring to coat. If beans seem dry, add reserved cooking liquid as needed. Add salt and adjust seasoning to taste. reheat gently and keep warm until ready to serve.

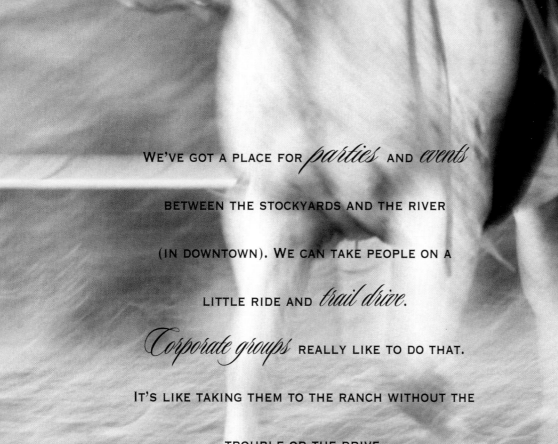

WE'VE GOT A PLACE FOR *parties* AND *events*

BETWEEN THE STOCKYARDS AND THE RIVER

(IN DOWNTOWN). WE CAN TAKE PEOPLE ON A

LITTLE RIDE AND *trail drive*.

Corporate groups REALLY LIKE TO DO THAT.

IT'S LIKE TAKING THEM TO THE RANCH WITHOUT THE

TROUBLE OR THE DRIVE.

—Steve Murrin
River Ranch and West Fork Ranch,
Fort Worth, Texas

1½ CUPS SUGAR, DIVIDED USE

5 EGGS, WELL-BEATEN

1 13-OUNCE CAN EVAPORATED MILK

1 CUP HEAVY CREAM

2 TEASPOONS VANILLA

makes 8 servings

FLAN

There's simply no better dessert than flan—
egg custard with caramel syrup—no matter what the meal.

Sprinkle ½ cup sugar over bottom of a 9-inch non-reactive metal cake pan and place over medium heat. Cook, stirring constantly, until sugar melts and turns a caramel (golden) brown. Remove from heat. Turn pan to coat bottom and sides evenly. Allow to cool. In a medium mixing bowl, combine ¾ cup sugar, eggs, evaporated milk, cream and vanilla, blending well. Pour over caramel in pan.

Place pan with flan in a larger pan. Place in oven. Pour enough hot water into larger pan to come up the side of flan pan about 1 inch. Bake for 55 to 60 minutes or until a knife inserted near the center comes out clean. Center will jiggle but should not appear fluid.

Remove from oven and lift flan pan from water. Cool for 10 to 15 minutes. Invert onto a serving dish with a rim. The caramel will form a sauce on top of the baked custard.

RODEO COWBOYS

Rodeos began as ranch competitions among working cowboys. Today, however, rodeo is a sport with professional superstars who vie for championships on a rodeo circuit, similar to a Professional Golf Association tour.

Just as today's hockey players don't have to learn their trade on a frozen lake, rodeo cowboys don't necessarily develop their skills on the ranch. There are professional rodeo schools to develop techniques and timing for bull and bronc riding, calf roping, and steer wrestling. Trainers work with horses and riders to perfect the right moves for barrel racing.

Today's cowboys—and the animals they ride—are professional athletes, training virtually year-round. Watching cowboys prepare for their bronc or bull rides behind the chutes is like watching athletes in other sports warm up and stretch. Rodeoing is a rough sport, and many cowboys wrap or pad ankles, knees, ribs, or shoulders to protect against injury. In recent years, cowboys have begun wearing flak jackets and football helmets to protect themselves from serious injury.

No matter whether on a ranch or in town, rodeo cowboys—like traditional cowboys—usually prefer simple cooking. The following recipes are the stuff of home- and country-cooking restaurants where cowboys often find a bite to eat on the drives between rodeo venues.

CHICKEN-FRIED STEAK

*There's not a cowboy anywhere who wouldn't rather have a
chicken fried steak with cream gravy than just about anything.
That dish is as symbolic of cowboys as apple pie is of the
good ol' USA. This version is the real homemade style with
a relatively delicate crust—country tempura, if you please—not
one of the pre-fab coatings that can withstand freezing,
shipping, and a quick dip in hot, deep fat. If you go to the
trouble to make chicken-fried steak at home, go the whole
distance: make cream gravy, too.*

4 TO 6 TENDERIZED BEEF CUTLETS OR
1 TO 1½ POUNDS BEEF OR VENISON
ROUND STEAK, CUT INTO 4 TO
6 SERVING-SIZE PIECES

1 CUP MILK

1 EGG, LIGHTLY BEATEN

1½ CUPS FLOUR

1 TEASPOON SALT OR TO TASTE

1 TEASPOON PEPPER OR TO TASTE

2 CUPS VEGETABLE OIL OR AS NEEDED

CREAM GRAVY (SEE RECIPE ON
PAGE 77)

Rinse and dry beef cutlets or round steak. If using round steak, pound each piece with a meat mallet to tenderize. Combine milk and egg in a shallow bowl. Add meat to bowl, turning to coat all sides. Allow to marinate for about 30 minutes.

Stir together flour, salt and pepper in a shallow bowl or on a plate. Remove meat from milk, allowing excess to drip back into bowl. Dredge meat in flour, turning to coat all sides evenly.

For a thicker crust, dip each piece of meat back in milk, then coat again with flour. If needed, add additional milk to coat remaining pieces. After one or two coatings, place each battered piece in a single layer on a large sheet of wax paper.

Pour enough vegetable oil into a heavy-bottom skillet to a depth of 1 inch. Heat over medium high heat to 375°. When oil is hot, carefully slide beef into hot oil, one piece at a time. Wait a minute or so for oil to come back to desired heat level. Cook 2 or 3 pieces of meat at a time. Do not crowd skillet.

When bottom crust is golden brown, about 3 to 5 minutes cooking time, carefully turn to cook other side. Cook until golden brown and place on paper towel to drain. Keep warm while cooking remaining pieces of meat. Serve hot with Cream Gravy.

*Chicken-fried chicken:
Substitute boneless, skinless
chicken breasts for beef or venison.
Pound to flatten to an even thickness.
Marinade in milk, coat with seasoned
flour and fry as above.*

makes 4 to 6 servings

VARIATION: BATTER-FRIED JALAPEÑOS FOR CHICKEN-FRIED STEAK. THIS IS PARTICULARLY GOOD
IF USING VENISON ROUND STEAK. DRAIN 1 8-OUNCE CAN OR JAR SLICED, PICKLED JALAPEÑOS.
PLACE DRAINED JALAPEÑOS IN MILK ALONG WITH ROUND STEAK. USE ADDITIONAL MILK, IF NEEDED.
MARINATE PEPPERS WITH MEAT AS ABOVE, REMOVE FROM MILK, SHAKE OFF EXCESS, AND COAT WITH
FLOUR. PLACE ON WAX PAPER. FRY STEAKS FIRST. WHEN STEAKS ARE BROWN AND CRISP, CAREFULLY
EASE BATTERED PEPPERS INTO HOT OIL, COOKING UNTIL GOLDEN, 2 TO 3 MINUTES. DRAIN ON PAPER
TOWELS AND KEEP WARM WITH BEEF WHILE PREPARING GRAVY.

LIVER AND ONIONS

Babies often grow up to be cowboys—and to like liver and onions.

In a large heavy-bottom skillet, heat 2 tablespoons oil over medium heat. Add onion rings and cook until edges are brown. Stir in sherry or sherry vinegar, if desired, and cook 1 to 2 minutes longer. Remove from pan and keep warm.

Lightly coat liver with flour on all sides, shaking off excess. Add 1 tablespoon (each) butter and oil to skillet. When bubbly, carefully place liver in hot butter-oil mixture and cook 1 to 2 minutes per side, turning once. Liver should be pink inside. Keep warm while cooking remaining slices, adding equal parts butter and oil as needed. Season cooked liver with salt and pepper to taste. Top with onions.

4 TABLESPOONS VEGETABLE OIL, DIVIDED USE

2 CUPS THINLY SLICED ONION RINGS, LOOSELY PACKED

½ CUP FLOUR

4 TABLESPOONS BUTTER, DIVIDED USE

1½ POUNDS CALF'S LIVER, SLICED ¼-INCH THICK

1 TEASPOON SALT OR TO TASTE

1 TEASPOON PEPPER OR TO TASTE

¼ CUP SHERRY OR 1 TABLESPOON SHERRY VINEGAR, OPTIONAL

makes 4 to 6 servings

1 6- TO 7-OUNCE BONE-IN RIBEYE
  PER PERSON, ABOUT ¾ INCH THICK

1 TEASPOON SALT, PEPPER AND PAPRIKA
  TO TASTE

¼ TO ½ CUP WATER

LEMON-GARLIC BUTTER SAUCE

PAN-GRILLED
BONE-IN RIBEYE STEAKS

*You may have to find a custom butcher to cut these bone-in
ribeye steaks for you, but you'll think they're worth it.
Steaks like this used to be weeknight fare in ranch households.
Now they're pretty special.*

Thirty minutes before cooking, remove steaks from refrigerator. Generously season on both sides with salt, pepper and paprika.

Heat 1 or 2 heavy-bottom skillets, preferably cast iron, over medium-high heat. Spray skillets with cooking spray. When skillets are hot, cook steaks, one at a time. Sear one side, turn and sear second side. Lower heat to medium and cook to desired degree, medium rare to medium. About 3 to 5 minutes

Remove steaks and keep warm. Add ¼ cup water to each skillet. Stir and cook over medium heat, scraping bottom to release any bits stuck to the pan. Cook until liquid is reduced by half. Pour over steaks just before serving, along with lemon-garlic butter sauce.

LEMON-GARLIC BUTTER SAUCE

½ CUP UNSALTED BUTTER

2 CLOVES GARLIC, MASHED

½ TEASPOON SALT OR TO TASTE

JUICE FROM ½ FRESH LEMON OR TO TASTE

In small saucepan, melt butter over low heat. Mash garlic with salt until it forms a paste. Stir garlic paste into hot butter and cook over low heat for 3 to 4 minutes. Remove garlic and discard if desired. Whisk in lemon juice. Pour over steaks and pass any remaining sauce.

makes enough sauce for 4 steaks
recipe doubles easily

COUNTRY POT ROAST
with PAN GRAVY

*A beef pot roast will make a cowboy come on home when
the lure of the rodeo arena makes him want to stay
on the road for another week . . . or two.
Try it and don't forget the gravy and mashed potatoes.*

Preheat oven to 300°. Rinse and dry roast. Combine flour, salt and pepper. Rub into all sides of roast. In a heavy-bottom Dutch oven, heat oil over medium heat. Add roast and brown on all sides, turning as needed.

When roast is brown, add water or beef broth, bay leaf, tomato paste, and balsamic vinegar or soy sauce. Bring liquid to a boil over high heat. Remove pan from heat, cover and place in oven for 30 to 45 minutes per pound or until roast is tender.

Remove from oven and allow to cool slightly. Carefully lift roast from pan and set aside. Remove and discard bay leaf. With a whisk, stir dissolved cornstarch into pan juices. Heat until sauce thickens to desired consistency. Pour any juices that accumulate around roast back into pan.

Slice roast thin and serve with plenty of pan gravy.

1 3- TO 4-POUND BEEF ROUND OR
   CHUCK TENDER ROAST

½ CUP FLOUR

1 TEASPOON SALT OR TO TASTE

1 TEASPOON PEPPER OR TO TASTE

1 TABLESPOON VEGETABLE OR OLIVE OIL

1 CUP WATER OR BEEF BROTH,
   AS NEEDED

1 BAY LEAF

1 TABLESPOON TOMATO PASTE

1 TABLESPOON BALSAMIC VINEGAR OR
   SOY SAUCE, OPTIONAL

1 TO 2 TABLESPOONS CORN STARCH
   MIXED WITH 1 TO 2 TABLESPOONS
   WATER

makes 6 to 8 servings

2 TO 4 POUNDS DRUMSTICKS, THIGHS
AND BONE-IN BREAST HALVES; MAY
ALSO USE CHICKEN TENDERS OR
BONELESS, SKINLESS BREASTS
(ENOUGH FOR 8 SERVINGS)*

1 QUART BUTTERMILK

1 CUP ALL-PURPOSE FLOUR

1 TEASPOON PAPRIKA

2 TEASPOONS SALT

2 TEASPOONS BLACK PEPPER

2 TO 4 CUPS VEGETABLE OIL OR
AS NEEDED

*Tip: To test the oil,
drop in a small piece of bread.
If grease is hot enough, the bread
will hit the oil, rise, float and turn
brown, almost immediately.*

*NOTE: IF USING CHICKEN TENDERS OR SKINLESS,
BONELESS BREASTS, FOLLOW PROCEDURE AS FOR
BONE-IN FRYER PIECES. SOAKING ISN'T NECESSARY
FOR TENDERS. RINSE, DIP IN BUTTERMILK, COAT
WITH FLOUR AND FRY IN HOT OIL, TURNING, UNTIL
ALL SIDES ARE BROWN. DRAIN ON PAPER TOWELS.

makes 8 servings

REAL HOME-FRIED CHICKEN

*Back before fast food made fried chicken one of the
easiest meals around, it was a labor of love and cowboys'
mamas knew how to do it right.
Heck, they could even cut a whole chicken into frying pieces.
But we won't go that far. Go ahead and use chicken pieces,
even boneless breasts or tenders if you like.
Just remember, the nearer the bone, the sweeter the meat.
Real cowboy mamas fry bone-in chicken.*

Rinse the chicken and pat dry. Place in a resealable plastic bag or shallow, flat, nonreactive baking dish and pour over enough buttermilk to cover. Refrigerate 1 hour, up to overnight.

Combine flour, paprika, salt, and pepper in a resealable plastic bag; shake to mix well. Remove chicken from buttermilk, shaking off excess. Place chicken in bag with flour, 1 or 2 pieces at a time, depending on size. Shake to coat evenly. Place on a sheet of wax paper while coating remaining pieces with flour.

Place a heavy-bottom skillet with high sides (preferably cast iron) over medium-high heat. Add 2 inches of oil. Heat until oil is hot, about 375°. Two pans may be needed if time is of the essence, since you shouldn't cook more then 3 or 4 pieces at a time so pan isn't crowded.

When oil is hot, begin with dark meat pieces such as thighs and legs because they take longer to cook. Cook breasts next. Carefully slide pieces into hot oil. When one piece floats, add another. Make sure sides do not touch.

Fry chicken until golden on one side. Reduce heat to about 325°, turn and fry until other side browns, about 15 to 20 minutes for dark meat pieces—10 to 15 for white meat. If desired, cover with lid during part of frying time.

Chicken is done when juices run clear. Check dark meat by piercing in the thickest part of the chicken nearest a joint. Drain on paper towels and keep warm while frying remaining chicken. Serve with Cream Gravy, if desired. (See page 71.)

3 LARGE BAKING POTATOES

1 TO 2 TEASPOONS SALT OR TO TASTE,
  DIVIDED USE

2 TO 3 TABLESPOONS BUTTER

1 CUP WARM MILK OR AS NEEDED

1 TEASPOON PEPPER OR TO TASTE

MOM'S MASHED POTATOES

*All that stuff about homemade mashed potatoes
with potato skins is bunk. No cowboy's mom was ever so
lazy that she didn't peel the potatoes.
Just wouldn't be right.*

Peel potatoes and cut each into 8 pieces. Place in a large pot or saucepan with enough cold water to cover. Add 1 teaspoon salt or to taste. Place over high heat and bring to a boil. Reduce heat to a low boil, cover and cook until potatoes are tender and easily pierced with a fork, about 15 minutes.

Drain potatoes in a colander. Return potatoes to the saucepan and place over low heat for 1 to 2 minutes, shaking frequently, to steam away excess liquid for fluffier mashed potatoes.

Remove from heat. Using a potato masher, begin mashing potatoes. Add butter and continue mashing until potatoes are in small pieces. Using electric beater, gradually beat warm milk into potatoes to achieve desired consistency. Add pepper and adjust salt as needed.

makes 6 servings

POLITE COMPANY PINTO BEANS

See Ranchhand Pinto Beans on page 14. For pinto beans that are a bit easier to digest, however, omit garlic and jalapeño from the beans and add ½ teaspoon ground ginger.

MACARONI AND CHEESE

For many cowboys, a vegetarian plate consists of pinto beans, macaroni cheese, fried okra and corn. Some folks might consider this a little heavy on the fried foods and starches; most cowboys just know they're going without a hunk of meat. Compensation, after all, must be made.

8 OUNCES LARGE OR REGULAR MACARONI

1 TABLESPOON BUTTER

1 TEASPOON YELLOW MUSTARD

1 EGG, LIGHTLY BEATEN

½ TEASPOON SALT OR TO TASTE

3 CUPS (ABOUT 12 OUNCES) GRATED CHEDDAR CHEESE, DIVIDED USE

2 TABLESPOONS FLOUR

1¾ CUPS MILK

Preheat oven to 325–350°. Spray a 2-quart casserole with cooking spray. Cook macaroni in large pot or saucepan according to package directions. Pasta should be tender, but not too soft. Drain well and allow to cool slightly. Return to saucepan.

Stir in butter, mustard, egg and salt. Add 2½ cups cheese and flour, mixing well. Turn mixture into prepared casserole dish. Pour milk over macaroni and cheese. Using the back of a spoon, press down macaroni so milk covers the pasta.

Bake for about 35 minutes or until bubbly. Sprinkle remaining cheese on top and bake about 10 minutes longer or until the custard is set and the top is golden and crusty.

This version of Macaroni and Cheese is easy to make because it omits the traditional cheese sauce step.

makes 8 servings

1 16-OUNCE PACKAGE FROZEN
   BLACK-EYED PEAS WITH SNAPS OR
   PURPLE HULL PEAS OR 1 PINT
   FRESH PEAS

1 CUP CHOPPED ONION

1 CUP CHICKEN OR VEGETABLE STOCK

2 STRIPS BACON, CUT INTO
   1-INCH PIECES, OPTIONAL

1 TEASPOON SALT OR TO TASTE

1 TEASPOON PEPPER OR TO TASTE

makes 8 servings

2 EGGS

1 CUP MILK

2 TEASPOONS BUTTER

½ CUP CHOPPED ONION

1 TEASPOON SALT OR TO TASTE

½ TEASPOON WHITE PEPPER OR TO TASTE

1 8-OUNCE CAN CREAM-STYLE CORN

2 CUPS FRESH OR FROZEN
   WHOLE KERNEL CORN

½ CUP CHOPPED FRESH PARSLEY

makes 6 to 8 servings

BLACK-EYED PEAS

Combine black-eyed peas, onion, stock, and bacon in a medium saucepan over medium heat. Bring liquid to a boil, reduce heat to simmer. Cover saucepan and cook until peas are tender, about 30 to 45 minutes, depending on preferred texture. Make sure too much liquid does not cook away. Black-eyed peas should be almost, but not quite, covered with liquid. When peas are tender, add salt and pepper to taste.

To use dried black-eyed peas:
Soak 2 cups peas in enough water to cover overnight. Drain soaking water and proceed as above using 4 cups stock or water. Do not add salt until peas are soft. Increase cooking time to 1½ hours or until tender. Check to make sure liquid does not evaporate during cooking. Add salt and pepper to taste.

CORN PUDDING

This dish is as warm and homey as grandma's lap and almost as soft. Serve Corn Pudding with pork or chicken.

Preheat oven to 325°. Spray a 1½-quart casserole with cooking spray or lightly coat with butter. Heat butter in a small skillet or saucepan over medium heat. Add onion and cook until onions are soft. Remove from heat and allow to cool slightly. In a medium bowl, beat together eggs, milk, salt, and white pepper. Fold in onions, cream-style corn, whole kernel corn, and parsley.

Pour into casserole. Place in oven and bake 30 to 40 minutes or until bubbly at the edges and set in the center. A toothpick inserted in the center should come out clean.

I'VE TRAVELED A LOT IN THE

American West AND BECAME ENTHRALLED WITH

THE FOOD BECAUSE IT IS SO *fresh* AND *vibrant*.

WE LOVE *rafting trips,*

flyfishing,

horseback riding

AND A LOT OF THE DISHES WE DID ON THESE TRIPS

I'VE BROUGHT INDOORS WITHOUT SACRIFICING

THE *integrity* OF WHAT THE FOOD WAS ABOUT.

I'M TRYING TO BE VERY *purist,*

USING THE INGREDIENTS INDIGENOUS

TO THE *American West.*

—*Robert McGrath*

chef-owner of the Roaring Fork restaurant,

Scottsdale, Arizona

1½ CUPS LONG GRAIN WHITE RICE

3 CUPS WATER OR CHICKEN STOCK

4 OUNCES BULK PORK SAUSAGE OR
GROUND BEEF

1 CUP CHOPPED ONION

1 CUP CHOPPED GREEN BELL PEPPER OR
COMBINATION RED AND GREEN
BELL PEPPER

½ TEASPOON RED PEPPER FLAKES,
OPTIONAL

1 TEASPOON SALT OR TO TASTE

1 TEASPOON BLACK PEPPER OR TO TASTE

makes 6 servings

8 EGGS

1 CUP MILK

½ TEASPOON SALT OR TO TASTE

½ TEASPOON BLACK PEPPER OR TO TASTE

2 4-OUNCE CANS CHOPPED GREEN
CHILIES (DRAINED) OR 1 CUP CHOPPED
FRESH ROASTED GREEN CHILIES
(SEE PAGE 41)

1½ CUP SHREDDED MONTEREY JACK OR
CHEDDAR CHEESE, OR A COMBINATION

makes 8 servings

DIRTY RICE

*Cowboys with a taste for Cajun cooking find this
dish particularly rewarding.
It's almost meatless, at least by cowboy standards.*

Combine rice, water, or chicken stock and ½ teaspoon salt in a 2-quart microwave-safe dish. Cover and place in microwave. Cook on high power for 5 minutes. Lower heat to 50 percent power and cook for 15 to 18 minutes or until liquid is absorbed. Remove from microwave, fluff rice with a fork and set aside.

Crumble sausage into a large skillet over medium-high heat. Cook, using the back of a spoon to break sausage or ground beef into small pieces, until meat begins to brown, about 3 minutes. Reduce heat to low and add onions, stirring occasionally. When onions begin to soften, after 3 to 5 minutes, add bell pepper and cook 2 to 3 minutes longer or until bell pepper begins to wilt. For a spicier dish, add red pepper flakes.

Fold sausage or beef mixture into rice. Cover and microwave 2 to 3 minutes longer to heat through.

GREEN CHILIES *and* EGGS

*Whether it is for breakfast or as a side dish,
this recipe is so good it can make a cowboy cry.*

Preheat oven to 325°. Spray a 9 x 9-inch glass baking dish with cooking spray. Break eggs into a medium bowl. Beat lightly. Beat in 1 cup milk, along with salt and pepper. Fold in green chilies and cheese. Pour into prepared baking dish. Place in oven for 30 to 35 minutes or until eggs are set. Cut into squares and serve hot.

GREEN BEANS
with SWEET ONIONS

*Use Kentucky Wonder or any kind of snap beans for this
homestyle way of cooking. For a rare spring treat
(if you can find them), substitute pods of immature pinto beans.
Not quite as sweet as snow peas, they're similar in
appearance and very tender.*

Rinse green beans. Cut or snap off stem end. Cut or break into 2-inch
lengths. Rinse again and drain. Place bacon in a large saucepan over medium heat. Cook until bacon begins to soften and about 1 tablespoon fat
melts. Or heat 1 tablespoon olive oil in saucepan.

Add onion and cook until onion is soft, about 5 minutes. Do not
brown. Add green beans, stirring to coat with bacon fat or oil and combine with onions. Add water to almost cover beans. Bring liquid to a boil,
reduce heat and cook at a low boil for 8 minutes.

Reduce heat, place cover on beans and simmer until easily pierced with
a fork, 5 to 10 minutes, depending on type of bean and tenderness desired.
Some cowboys like really soft, almost mushy, green beans. Add sugar or
syrup during last few minutes of cooking. Add salt and pepper to taste.

With New Potatoes: Rinse and scrub 1 pound new (red) potatoes. Cut
into halves or fourths, depending on size. Place in medium saucepan with
enough cold water to cover. Add 1 teaspoon salt. Over high heat, bring
water to a boil. Lower heat, cover and simmer 10 to 12 minutes or until
potatoes are easily pierced with fork. Drain potatoes and add to cooked
green beans.

With Caramelized Sweet Onion Chutney: Slice 2 sweet onions into
thinnest rings possible. Heat 1 tablespoon oil and 1 tablespoon butter in
large, heavy-bottom skillet over low heat. Add onions, stirring to coat
with oil and butter. Lay a piece of wax paper directly on onions and place
lid on skillet. Cook until very soft, about 10 minutes. Check occasionally,
reducing heat as needed to prevent browning. Sprinkle ¼ cup sugar over
onions. Cook, uncovered, until onions and sugar begin to brown and
caramelize. Continue cooking over lowest heat until liquid is reduced and
syrupy. Stir in 1 to 2 teaspoons balsamic vinegar. Season to taste with salt.
Garnish each serving of green beans with a dollop of chutney.

1 POUND FRESH GREEN BEANS
(OR YOUNG PINTO BEAN PODS)

2 STRIPS BACON, CUT IN 1-INCH STRIPS
OR 1 TABLESPOON OLIVE OIL

1 CUP CHOPPED SWEET ONION

1 TO 1½ CUPS WATER OR AS NEEDED

1 TEASPOON SUGAR OR
PURE MAPLE SYRUP

1 TEASPOON SALT OR TO TASTE

1 TEASPOON BLACK PEPPER OR TO TASTE

makes 4 to 6 servings

1 BUNCH (EACH) TURNIP, COLLARD AND
  MUSTARD GREENS

1 TO 2 CUPS CHICKEN STOCK OR WATER

3 TO 4 STRIPS BACON, CUT IN 1-INCH
  PIECES

1 TO 2 TABLESPOONS SUGAR, OR TO
  TASTE

  BOTTLED VINEGAR PEPPER SAUCE

makes 10 servings

MIXED GREENS

Clean greens well. To remove traces of sand and grit, tear off thick stems and place greens in the sink. Cover with water. Sprinkle a small amount of salt over greens and stir. Let rest for 5 minutes so any sand settles to the bottom of the sink. Carefully lift out greens and place in a colander or large bowl.

Rinse out sink to eliminate any grit that may have dropped from greens. Return greens to sink and cover with water again. After 5 more minutes, unplug drain to release water. Without shaking off too much water, tear large leaves into pieces and place in a large stockpot or saucepan with a lid. Discard thickest stems. Add greens and bacon to pan in layers.

Pack greens in tightly, cover and place over medium heat. Cook just until leaves wilt and collapse. Add just enough water or chicken stock to almost cover greens. Bring liquid to a boil, reduce heat and simmer, covered, until greens are tender, about 30 minutes. Stir in sugar during last 10 minutes of cooking. Season each serving with vinegar pepper sauce.

1 16-OUNCE PACKAGE FROZEN CUT OKRA

1¼ CUPS YELLOW CORNMEAL

½ CUP FLOUR

1 TEASPOON SALT OR TO TASTE

1 TEASPOON BLACK PEPPER OR TO TASTE

2 CUPS VEGETABLE OIL OR AS NEEDED

makes 4 to 6 servings

FRIED OKRA

*Using frozen okra makes for a thicker batter that better
adheres to this notoriously slimy vegetable.
Not to worry: frying cuts this texture.*

Empty frozen okra into a large bowl of cold water to thaw. Meanwhile, combine cornmeal, flour, salt, and pepper in a large plastic bag. In a heavy bottom saucepan or deep fryer, heat oil (should be 2 inches deep) to 350°.

When thawed, lift okra out of water using a slotted spoon. Drain thoroughly, then drop into seasoned cornmeal. Add 2 or 3 spoonfuls to bag at one time. Shake to coat okra. Carefully place okra, separating pieces, in hot oil. Okra should float immediately and turn golden in 2 to 3 minutes. Remove and drain on paper towels; keep warm.

Repeat steps with remaining okra. Serve immediately.

CREAM GRAVY

*For the best cream gravy,
use the same skillet used for chicken-fried steak or
fried chicken. Pour off all but 3 tablespoons of the
frying oil—that way you get all of those tasty bits that
are stuck to the bottom of the pan in the gravy.
That's the way cowboys' moms do it.*

Heat oil or drippings in large skillet over medium heat. Stir in flour and cook until bubbly, scraping up any bits that may stick to bottom of pan. Add milk and water, stirring constantly with wire whisk or the back of a slotted spoon. Lower heat and simmer until thickened. Add salt and pepper to taste. Serve over chicken-fried steak, mashed potatoes or just about any meat or fowl, particularly if it is fried.

3 TABLESPOONS VEGETABLE OIL OR DRIPPINGS FROM FRYING PAN

¼ CUP FLOUR

1 CUP (EACH) WARM MILK AND WARM WATER, MORE LIQUID IF NEEDED

1 TEASPOON SALT OR TO TASTE

1 TEASPOON PEPPER OR TO TASTE

makes 6 to 8 servings

SKILLET CORNBREAD

*Making cornbread in a cast-iron skillet tastes
great and looks authentic. So why not?*

Preheat oven to 425°. Generously grease a 10-inch cast-iron skillet (or a 9 x 9-inch square baking pan) and heat in oven while mixing batter.

Stir together cornmeal, flour, baking powder, sugar, and salt in a large bowl. In small bowl, combine beaten eggs, oil and milk. Pour into cornmeal mixture and mix just to blend ingredients. Do not overbeat.

Remove pan from oven and pour batter into hot pan. Bake 20 to 25 minutes until edges are golden and pull away from sides of pan. The center should be set.

1¼ CUPS YELLOW CORNMEAL

¾ CUP ALL-PURPOSE FLOUR, PREFERABLY UNBLEACHED

2 TEASPOONS BAKING POWDER

1 TEASPOON SUGAR

¾ TEASPOON SALT

2 EGGS, LIGHTLY BEATEN

2 TABLESPOONS VEGETABLE OIL

1 CUP MILK

makes 10 to 12 servings

When people think of *cowboys*, they often think of 10-gallon hats,

roping and rodeos. But, to me, being a *cowboy* is

more than just a performance. It's a way of life.

It's about *digging in*, working smart and *never giving up*.

Have you ever stopped to notice the hands of a farmer or rancher?

They're *strong* and *rugged*, and they tell stories of

years spent working the earth and tending to livestock.

Persistence, dedication and the importance of neighbor

helping neighbor are things I learned from my father,

who was a rancher in West Texas. Sure, sometimes life

can be *rough riding*, but you have to *get up*,

brush off the dirt and *get right back on*.

And that's what I call having the *cowboy spirit*.

—*Susan V. Combs*

Texas Agriculture Commissioner,
Austin and Alpine, Texas

REFRIGERATOR DINNER ROLLS

*Big, yeasty rolls, fresh from the oven—nothing's better
to a cowboy coming home from a rodeo tour.
Best of all, this dough can be made ahead and stored in the
refrigerator for 2 to 3 days before baking. Nothing to it.*

Dissolve yeast in warm water, stirring to blend. Let stand 10 minutes. In a large mixing bowl, combine potato flakes, butter, eggs, salt and sugar, mixing well. Gradually blend in 3½ cups of flour. Stir in yeast mixture and begin kneading dough. Turn out onto lightly floured board and knead until smooth and shiny, about 10 minutes. Place in medium-size clean, well-greased bowl and cover bowl with a layer of plastic wrap and a kitchen towel. Dough may be stored 2 to 3 days.

Grease 3 12-muffin tins or a cookie sheet. Punch down dough and knead in an additional ½ cup flour or as needed so dough will hold a shape. Break off a golf ball-size piece of dough and shape into a round. Place in a greased muffin cup. Fill all muffin cups. If desired, place dough rounds on a greased cookie sheet, about 2 inches apart.

Cover rolls with a kitchen towel and place away from drafts. Let stand 2–3 hours or until doubled in size. To prepare rolls, preheat oven to 450°. Bake for 10 to 12 minutes or until golden brown.

1 ¼-OUNCE PACKAGE DRY YEAST

¾ CUP WARM WATER

½ CUP INSTANT MASHED POTATO FLAKES

½ CUP BUTTER, SOFTENED

2 EGGS

¾ TEASPOON SALT

½ CUP SUGAR

4 CUPS FLOUR OR AS NEEDED, DIVIDED USE

makes about 3 dozen rolls

4 EGGS

2 CUPS SUGAR

2 TABLESPOONS ALL-PURPOSE FLOUR

7 TABLESPOONS MELTED BUTTER (NOT
MARGARINE)

1¼ TEASPOONS VANILLA

¼ TEASPOON SALT

¾ CUP BUTTERMILK

1 (10-INCH) UNBAKED PIE SHELL (SEE
RECIPE BELOW)

1 CUP FRESH BLACKBERRIES

⅛ CUP CONFECTIONERS' SUGAR

MINT LEAVES, OPTIONAL

BUTTERMILK PIE WITH BLACKBERRIES

This pie makes for a smooth as doeskin ending to a big deal meal. Based on a family recipe from Gale Hearn Plummer of Dallas, this has been adapted over time and is a family favorite. Add some fresh blackberries for color and a tart zing.

Preheat oven to 350°. Place eggs in a medium bowl and beat until smooth but still frothy. Add sugar, flour, butter, vanilla, and salt. Mix thoroughly until dry ingredients are well-blended.

Gently blend in buttermilk being careful not to overbeat. Pour into pie shell.

To prevent crust from overbrowning, place strips of foil (or a 1-inch wide circle of foil) over crust just to edge of filling. Bake pie for 50 to 55 minutes or until filling is set. To test, insert a knife in center of filling; blade should come out clean and the middle should not jiggle. Remove from oven and cool completely.

Serve pie at room temperature or gently chilled.

About 30 minutes before serving, rinse blackberries and drain. Place in a small bowl and sprinkle with confectioners' sugar. Toss gently to coat berries evenly without bruising.

Garnish each serving with a spoonful of berries and a drizzle of accumulated juice. If desired, add a mint leaf or two for additional color.

Makes 8 servings.

makes 8 servings

PIE CRUST

Combine flour and salt in a large bowl, mixing well with fork or wooden spoon. Cut in shortening using a pastry blender or two knives. Flour should be fine and crumbly.

Add water 1 very full tablespoon at a time, mixing well with a fork after each addition. Finish blending crust using hands to form a ball. Wrap in plastic and refrigerate 30 minutes to 1 hour.

Lightly sprinkle a board with flour or cover board with pastry cloth and dust pastry cloth with flour. Place the dough on floured surface and flatten into a disc. Turn disc over to roll our floured side. Also dust rolling pin with flour.

Roll out dough to about 12 inches in diameter. Place dough into pie plate and flute or crimp edges. Fill with desired filling.

To bake crust before filling, preheat over to 400° F. Line pie plate with pastry and prick bottom and sides of pastry with a fork. Bake 7 to 8 minutes or just until pastry is light golden in color.

Makes enough for 1 (9- or 10-inch) crust.

1 ⅛ CUPS ALL-PURPOSE FLOUR (DO NOT USE UNBLEACHED)

½ TEASPOON SALT

½ CUP VEGETABLE SHORTENING

3 TABLESPOONS WATER

2 CUPS SUGAR, DIVIDED USE

⅓ CUP COCOA

7 TABLESPOONS CORNSTARCH

½ TEASPOON SALT, DIVIDED USE

3 EGGS, SEPARATED

2 CUPS MILK

2 TABLESPOONS BUTTER

2 TEASPOONS VANILLA

¼ TEASPOON CREAM OF TARTAR

1 BAKED 9-INCH PIE SHELL

makes 8 serving

CHOCOLATE MERINGUE PIE

*What's better than anything chocolate?
Homemade chocolate meringue pie.*

Preheat oven to 350°. In a medium saucepan, combine 1⅓ cups sugar, cocoa, cornstarch and ¼ teaspoon salt, blending well. Beat egg yolks until light yellow and combine with milk. Gradually add milk mixture to dry ingredients, stirring constantly with a wire whisk.

Place saucepan over medium-low heat and cook, stirring constantly, until the pudding comes to a low boil and thickens enough to coat the back of a spoon. Remove from heat and stir in butter and vanilla. Pour into baked pie shell.

Place egg whites in a medium bowl. Beat on high speed with electric beaters until foamy. Gradually add ¼ teaspoon salt, ⅔ cup sugar and cream of tartar, beating constantly, until meringue forms stiff peaks. Spread meringue over chocolate filling, spreading to the edges of the crust to seal the filling. Bake for 12 to 15 minutes, until peaks are light brown.

CITY COWBOYS

Cowboys and boots go together wherever they are. In fact, you can tell a lot about a cowboy by his boots. Some urban cowboys wear fancy boots—snake skin or brightly colored—to go line-dancing or to the annual barbecue festival. For others, conservative black boots, instead of wing tips, are everyday professional or workday attire.

While urban cowboys may never get mud on their boots, they likely long for a chance to get out and experience wide open spaces.

In turn, there's a whole genre of slicked-up cowboy food served at casual restaurants, sports bars, or wherever cowboy mystique is part of the atmosphere. The recipes in this chapter adapt many of these casual restaurant and barbecue joint favorites for home preparation.

½ POUND GROUND BEEF

2 TEASPOONS CHILI POWDER

1 TABLESPOON WATER

1 24-OUNCE BAG RESTAURANT-STYLE
TORTILLA CHIPS

1 16-OUNCE BAG GRATED
CHEDDAR CHEESE

1 12-OUNCE JAR OR CAN SLICED
JALAPEÑOS

1 8-OUNCE CAN REFRIED BEANS

2 CUPS SHREDDED, COOKED CHICKEN

1 CUP GUACAMOLE (SEE PAGE 99)

1 CUP SOUR CREAM

1 CUP RINGS SLICED FROM A
LARGE-DIAMETER ONION

makes 8 to 10 servings

NACHOS

*Whether they're an appetizer or a happy meal alongside
a pitcher of beer, nachos are the finger food of choice for
lots of cowboys. These are loaded. Of course,
simple nachos—cheese melted on crispy tortilla
fragments with sliced jalapeños—will do in a pinch.*

Heat a small skillet over medium heat. Crumble ground beef into skillet. Cook, stirring occasionally to break up pieces, until meat is no longer pink. Stir in chili powder and water. Reduce heat and simmer until liquid is evaporated. Set aside, off heat.

Preheat broiler. Arrange tortilla chips in a single layer on several baking sheets. Spread each tortilla chip with refried beans and a layer of grated cheese. Place nachos under broiler just until cheese melts, 3 to 5 minutes.

Spoon chicken or beef on each nacho. Top with a dollop of Guacamole and Pico de Gallo (see recipes on page 99), along with sour cream. Arrange jalapeño slices and onion rings over nachos. Serve immediately.

FAJITAS
(BEEF OR CHICKEN)

The origin of fajitas has been traced to the South Texas ranch culture where Mexican ranch hands made good use of one of the less tender cuts, called a skirt steak, a muscle that wraps the ribs. The literal meaning of the Spanish word is "little belt."
In today's parlance, fajita *means any meat, poultry, or seafood which is grilled, sliced and served in a flour tortilla.*

Rinse and dry chicken breasts or skirt steak. Place in a resealable plastic bag or in shallow glass dish. In a small bowl or measuring cup, whisk together oil, soy sauce, garlic, lime juice, black pepper, and pepper sauce. Pour marinade over chicken or beef. Cover and refrigerate 1 to 4 hours, turning occasionally so marinade soaks in evenly.

Prepare fire or preheat a gas grill to medium. When fire has burned down to medium or grill is preheated, drain marinade from chicken or beef and discard. Season chicken or beef to taste with salt and pepper. Grill chicken or beef over medium heat for 5 to 6 minutes per side (a bit less for medium-rare beef). Juices should run clear when chicken is pierced with a fork. Remove from fire and keep warm.

Saute onion rings and green pepper strips in 2 teaspoons vegetable oil in a skillet over high heat on the stove or in a skillet on the grill, until golden at the edges and wilted. Season to taste with salt and pepper. Keep warm.

Cut chicken or beef across the grain into thin diagonal slices. Serve with grilled onions and peppers, hot flour tortillas, salsa, pico de gallo, guacamole, and refried beans.

See how to wrap and eat fajitas, p. 87

To heat flour tortillas: Wrap tightly in foil and place in a 300° oven for 30 minutes or until tortillas are hot. A microwave tortilla warmer also works well. Follow manufacturer's instructions or line the microwave-safe warmer with a paper towel lightly sprinkled with water. Place tortillas in warmer with lid in place. Microwave on high for 1 to 2 minutes or until tortillas are hot, checking every 30 seconds.

1 TO 1½ POUNDS BONELESS, SKINLESS CHICKEN BREAST OR 1 (1¼- TO 1½-POUND) SKIRT STEAK*

½ CUP VEGETABLE OIL

1 TABLESPOON SOY SAUCE

3 CLOVES GARLIC, CRUSHED

⅓ CUP LIME JUICE OR THE JUICE OF 1 TO 2 LIMES

1 TEASPOON BLACK PEPPER

2 TO 3 DROPS RED PEPPER SAUCE OR TO TASTE, OPTIONAL

1 WHITE ONION, SLICED INTO THIN RINGS

1 GREEN BELL PEPPER, CUT INTO THIN STRIPS

SALT AND PEPPER TO TASTE

10 TO 12 HOT FLOUR TORTILLAS (SEE PAGE 45)

MI CASA SALSA (SEE PAGE 96)

PICO DE GALLO (SEE PAGE 99)

GUACAMOLE (SEE PAGE 99)

REFRIED BEANS (SEE PAGE 96)

Tip: Use half chicken and half beef, marinate in separate containers. Proceed as above.

*MAY SUBSTITUTE TENDERIZED ROUND STEAK

makes 4 to 6 servings

SHRIMP FAJITAS

*Use large shrimp for fajitas. They're not as likely
to overcook and dry out.*

Rinse and dry shrimp and place in a large resealable plastic bag or in a shallow glass baking dish. In a small bowl or measuring cup, whisk together oil, lime juice, garlic and cayenne pepper. Pour marinade over shrimp. Cover and refrigerate 30 minutes to 1 hour, turning occasionally.

Prepare fire or preheat a gas grill to medium. When fire has burned down to medium or grill is preheated, drain marinade from shrimp and discard. Season shrimp to taste with salt and pepper. Place shrimp in a single layer in a grill basket. Grill shrimp 1 to 2 minutes per side. Do not overcook. Remove from fire and keep warm.

Saute onion rings and green pepper strips in 2 teaspoons vegetable oil in a skillet over high heat on the stove or in a skillet on the grill, just until golden at the edges and wilted. Season to taste with salt and pepper. Keep warm.

If shrimp are very large, chop in large chunks. For more attractive presentation, leave shrimp whole. Serve with grilled onions and peppers, hot flour tortillas, salsa, pico de gallo, guacamole, and refried beans.

Tip: If shrimp are very large, use half the recommended amount and cut shrimp in half lengthwise.

How to wrap and eat fajitas: The idea with fajitas is to roll the filling and desired garnishes in a flour tortilla to make it easy to pick up and eat. The most practical way is to start with the soft stuff—like refried beans or guacamole—and spread them on the flour tortilla. Layer on fajita strips or shrimp and other garnishes—onions, green peppers, salsa or pico de gallo—as desired.

1 TO 1¼ POUNDS LARGE SHRIMP, SHELLS
  AND TAILS REMOVED

½ CUP VEGETABLE OIL

¼ CUP LIME JUICE OR THE JUICE OF
  1 LIME

1 CLOVE GARLIC, CRUSHED

¼ TEASPOON CAYENNE PEPPER OR
  TO TASTE

1 TEASPOON SALT OR TO TASTE,
  DIVIDED USE

1 TEASPOON PEPPER OR TO TASTE,
  DIVIDED USE

1 WHITE ONION, SLICED INTO
  THIN RINGS

1 GREEN BELL PEPPER, CUT INTO
  THIN STRIPS

2 TEASPOONS OIL

10 TO 12 HOT FLOUR TORTILLAS (SEE
  PAGE 45; HOW TO HEAT, P. 85)

MI CASA SALSA (SEE PAGE 96)

PICO DE GALLO (SEE PAGE 99)

GUACAMOLE (SEE PAGE 99)

Shortcut:
*Substitute bottled Italian dressing
for fajita marinade.*

makes 4 to 6 servings

1 8- TO 10-POUND WHOLE BEEF BRISKET, UNTRIMMED

2 TABLESPOONS GARLIC SALT

2 TABLESPOONS LEMON PEPPER

2 TABLESPOONS PAPRIKA

1 TABLESPOON SUGAR

Shortcut: Use favorite packaged barbecue seasoning mix or rub.

makes 8 to 10 servings

BARBECUE BRISKET

Brisket is the tour de force for barbecue cooks west of the Mississippi. Pork is the deal in the Deep South—but in cattle country, beef is the thing to cook on the grill. Properly barbecued beef brisket should be cooked over indirect heat—the smoke does most of the cooking—for hours, until the surface is almost black. Slices of barbecued brisket should have a pink "smoke ring" around the outer edge. This is the by-product of the smoke on the meat and not an indication that somehow, after 8 to 24 hours in a smoker, the meat is rare at the edge and fork tender in the middle.

Remove brisket from refrigerator about 1 hour before grilling. Combine garlic salt, lemon pepper, paprika, and sugar. Sprinkle over entire surface of meat, concentrating on the fat layer. Using fingers or the back of a spoon, rub or press seasoning into meat.

Cover and let meat come to room temperature. Meanwhile, prepare fire: Light wood and/or charcoal in the firebox or at the end of a barrel smoker opposite the end with the vent or chimney. Or light coals in a water smoker or preheat one side of a gas smoker/grill.

When fire has burned down to glowing embers or coals are covered with gray ash, place ribs at end of smoker near the chimney, not directly over the coals. If using a water smoker, place a full pan of water over the coals, then position grill. Place brisket on grill over water pan. If using a gas grill, place brisket on unlit side of grill. Temperature inside the grill should be between 225° and 250°. Add coals as needed or adjust grill controls to maintain temperature.

Place brisket fat side up on the grill. Close lid of cooker and allow to smoke for 1 hour per pound or until meat is tender and exterior is dark and crusty. A pink ring near the surface of the meat is called the smoke ring. It does not indicate meat is undercooked.

To serve, slice brisket across the grain into thin slices. Serve with Let Me Call You Sweet Hot Barbecue Sauce.

SWEET-HOT SMOKY RIBS

*Ribs are the exception to the beef rule west of the Mississippi.
Even cowboys prefer pork ribs to beef, but the cooking
technique is virtually the same. The key to smoky,
juicy and tender ribs is long, slow cooking.
It is the smoke, not the fire, that does the cooking
so don't place ribs directly over the heat source.*

Coat ribs generously with Basic Barbecue Rub. Press spices into meat with fingers or the back of a spoon.

Prepare fire: Light wood and/or charcoal in the firebox or at the end of a barrel smoker opposite the end with the vent or chimney. Or light coals in a water smoker or preheat one side of a gas smoker/grill.

When fire has burned down to glowing embers or coals are covered with gray ash, place ribs at end of smoker near the chimney—not directly over the coals. If using a water smoker, place a full pan of water over the coals, then position grill. Place ribs on grill over water pan. If using a gas grill, place ribs on unlit side of grill.

Temperature inside the grill should be between 225° and 250°. Add coals as needed to maintain temperature. Place ribs meaty side up on the grill. Close lid of cooker and allow to smoke for 2 to 3 hours or until cooked through and tender. After 1 hour, turn ribs. Turn again after 30 minutes. When done, ribs should be browned and crisp on the exterior, tender on the inside.

During last 20 minutes of cooking, lightly brush one side of ribs with sauce and cook directly over coals about 10 minutes to glaze the ribs. Turn and lightly brush other side. Cook directly over coals about 10 minutes longer, just until sauce sets and dries.

To serve, slice ribs between the bones into individual pieces. Serve with additional sauce on the side.

2 FULL RACKS OF MEATY PORK SPARERIBS

BASIC BARBECUE RUB (SEE PAGE 90)

LET ME CALL YOU SWEET HOT BARBECUE SAUCE (SEE PAGE 90)

makes 4 to 6 servings

2 TABLESPOONS SALT

2 TABLESPOONS PEPPER

2 TABLESPOONS PAPRIKA

2 TABLESPOONS GARLIC POWDER

2 TABLESPOONS SUGAR

makes about 1¼ cups

1¼ CUPS KETCHUP

2 TABLESPOONS WORCESTERSHIRE SAUCE

⅓ CUP LEMON JUICE

½ CUP DARK BROWN SUGAR

¼ CUP WATER

1 TABLESPOON YELLOW MUSTARD

1 CLOVE GARLIC, CRUSHED

¼ CUP BUTTER OR PAN DRIPPINGS FROM BARBECUE

makes about 3 cups

BASIC BARBECUE RUB

"Rub" is what you call the seasoning blend for barbecue. Sprinkle on a generous coating of the mixture and "rub" or pat it in with your hands. This, along with long, slow cooking and lots of smoke, gives you authentic Western barbecue flavor.

In an air-tight container with lid, combine salt, pepper, paprika, garlic powder, and sugar. Shake to mix well. Use to season ribs or brisket before barbecuing.

Shortcut: Use your favorite packaged barbecue seasoning mix or rub.

LET ME CALL YOU SWEET HOT BARBECUE SAUCE

With a hint of sweet and a short blast of hot, this barbecue sauce works on meats from pork ribs to beef and chicken.

Combine ketchup, Worcestershire sauce, lemon juice, brown sugar, mustard, water, and garlic in a medium saucepan. Place over very low heat and simmer, stirring occasionally, 1 hour. For really smoky flavor, place on the grill away from heat source for the last hour of smoking. Stir in butter or brisket drippings and cook 15 minutes longer. Serve with ribs or other barbecue.

Shortcut: Add 2 to 3 tablespoons barbecue pan drippings to 1 bottle barbecue sauce. Heat and serve.

I'M MERELY TRYING TO *perfect* WHAT WAS DONE RIGHT IN THE FIRST PLACE.

THE TRADITION IS GREAT, BUT *chuck wagon cooks* DID WHAT THEY

DID AND NOW THEY'RE GONE. WE'RE IN A DIFFERENT SITUATION

WITH *better equipment.* I GET THEIR IDEAS AND TRY TO WORK WITH

THEM—NOT TO CHANGE THEM, BUT TO PERFECT THEM.

WE'VE GOT *better control* OF THE FIRE, REFRIGERATION.

WE CAN FREEZE STUFF. I ONCE THOUGHT I'D BE A HERO AND COME UP

WITH A NEW WAY OF COOKING BEANS. I PUT BEANS IN SALT WATER AND

FROZE THEM. I WANTED THEM TO *absorb* THE SALT AND SPLIT OPEN WHEN

THAWED SO THEY'D COOK REAL FAST . . . AND NOT PRODUCE GAS.

It didn't work.

—Matt Martinez
chef-owner of Matt's Rancho Martinez and Matt's No Place,
Dallas

FRIED CHICKEN RANCH CAESAR

This is something a cowboy's girlfriend might eat and it is darn good. Combining a country favorite with a city staple, a fried chicken Caesar salad has become a favorite on many cowboys' tables.

4 CHICKEN-FRIED CHICKEN BREASTS
  (SEE PAGE 64)

1 CUP BUTTERMILK

¼ CUP MAYONNAISE

¼ CUP SOUR CREAM

¼ CUP SHREDDED PARMESAN CHEESE

1 TEASPOON WORCESTERSHIRE SAUCE

1 CLOVE GARLIC, FINELY CHOPPED,
  THEN SMASHED

¼ TEASPOON SALT OR TO TASTE

½ TEASPOON BLACK PEPPER OR TO TASTE

1 QUART TORN ROMAINE LEAVES OR
  FAVORITE SALAD GREENS

3 SLICES OF BACON, FRIED CRISP
  AND CRUMBLED

3 GREEN ONIONS, SLICED THIN,
  INCLUDING GREEN PARTS

1 4-OUNCE CAN SLICED BLACK OLIVES,
  DRAINED

1 CUP SEEDED TOMATOES,
  FINELY CHOPPED

2 HARD-COOKED EGGS, SLICED THIN

Prepare Chicken-Fried Chicken Breasts; set aside. Or heat frozen batter-fried chicken tenders according to package directions.

In a medium bowl, combine buttermilk, mayonnaise, sour cream, Parmesan cheese, Worcestershire sauce and garlic. Stir to combine. Taste for seasoning; add salt and black pepper to taste; set aside. In a large salad bowl, toss about half the dressing with the salad greens, adding more as needed to coat greens well.

Assemble individual servings by dividing dressed salad greens among four plates. Cut each chicken breast into 4 to 6 slices. Lay slices from each breast over greens on each plate.

Garnish attractively with bacon, onion, olives, tomatoes, egg slices and a final dollop of dressing. Shake a very light dusting of cayenne pepper or paprika overall.

makes 4 servings

CHEESE ENCHILADAS

A good enchilada plate—cheese enchiladas with chili gravy,
refried beans and Mexican rice—is a staple in cowboy cafes
from Texas to the Rocky Mountains.

FOR CHILI GRAVY:

2 TABLESPOONS SHORTENING

2 TABLESPOONS FLOUR

2 TABLESPOONS CHILI POWDER

2 CUPS WARM WATER PLUS 1 8-OUNCE CAN TOMATO SAUCE

1 TEASPOON SALT OR TO TASTE

½ TEASPOON PEPPER OR TO TASTE

FOR FILLING:

4 CUPS GRATED LONGHORN OR CHEDDAR CHEESE

1 CUP FINELY CHOPPED ONION

12 CORN TORTILLAS (SEE PAGE 47)

2 TABLESPOONS COOKING OIL

In large skillet over medium heat, melt shortening and stir in flour. Cook until bubbly. Add chili powder and cook 1 minute. Stir in water and tomato sauce. Reduce heat so liquid simmers. Stir occasionally and cook until thickened, about 15 to 20 minutes. Add salt and pepper to taste; set aside, off heat.

Preheat oven to 350°. Lightly coat a 9 x 13-inch glass baking dish with nonstick cooking spray. Ready the ingredients in assembly line fashion: chili gravy, cheese and onions and tortillas.

Place cooking oil in small skillet over medium heat. Dip a tortilla in hot oil until softened, about 15 seconds. Allow excess grease to drain back into skillet. Then dip tortilla in chili gravy and place the tortilla in the baking dish.

Place about 3 to 4 tablespoons cheese and 1 to 2 teaspoons chopped onion down the middle of the tortilla. Roll tortilla to enclose filling and place seam side down.

Continue filling and rolling to make 12 tortillas. Arrange tortillas so they fit snugly in pan. Pour chili gravy over tortillas and sprinkle with remaining cheese and onion. Bake until bubbly, 15 to 20 minutes.

makes 12 enchiladas,
4 to 6 servings

MEXICAN RICE

This is the kind of rice you get in Mexican restaurants.
It is a meal in itself with refried beans and tortillas
and it's a must with enchiladas.

Drain tomatoes, setting aside liquid in a large measuring cup. Use the back of a wooden spoon or edge of a knife to break tomatoes into bite-size pieces; set aside.

Heat oil in a large skillet over medium heat. Add rice, stirring frequently, and cook until rice begins to brown. Add onion and carrots and cook until onions begin to soften. Lower heat, if necessary, to prevent rice from getting too dark. Stir in garlic.

To reserved tomato liquid, add beef or chicken stock and enough water to make three cups. Pour liquid into rice. Stir in crushed tomatoes, green chilies (or peppers), cumin, salt and pepper. Bring liquid to a boil. Reduce heat, cover and simmer until rice is tender and liquid is absorbed, about 20 to 25 minutes.

1 16-OUNCE CAN WHOLE TOMATOES, INCLUDING LIQUID

1 TABLESPOON VEGETABLE OIL OR BACON DRIPPINGS

1½ CUPS LONG-GRAIN RICE

1 CUP CHOPPED ONION

½ CUP FINELY CHOPPED CARROTS

2 CLOVES GARLIC, FINELY CHOPPED

1 4-OUNCE CAN CHOPPED GREEN CHILIES, DRAINED, OR 3 TABLESPOONS FINELY CHOPPED GREEN BELL PEPPER

½ TEASPOON CUMIN POWDER

1 14½-OUNCE CAN CHICKEN OR BEEF STOCK

1 TEASPOON SALT OR TO TASTE

½ TEASPOON PEPPER OR TO TASTE

makes 6 to 8 servings
this recipe doubles easily

4 CUPS RANCHHAND PINTO BEANS (SEE
PAGE 14), INCLUDING COOKING LIQUID
OR 2 17-OUNCE CANS REFRIED BEANS

1 CUP FINELY CHOPPED ONION

2 TABLESPOONS VEGETABLE OIL OR
BACON DRIPPINGS

½ TEASPOON SALT OR TO TASTE,
AS NEEDED

¼ TEASPOON PEPPER OR TO TASTE

makes 8 servings

REFRIED BEANS

The best refried beans use lard—and plenty of it—for "refrying"
or thinning and flavoring mashed pinto beans.
Please feel free to use it since no cookbook author dares
to actually list lard in a recipe these days—but really
good refried beans are made with lard.

If using whole, cooked pinto beans, use a potato masher or the back of a spoon to mash the beans. Add enough liquid so they make a thick, lumpy paste; set aside. If using canned refried beans, open can and set beans aside.

Heat oil or bacon drippings in a medium skillet over medium heat. Add onion and cook until wilted and brown at the edges, about 3 to 4 minutes. Add beans, stirring to mix well. Lower heat and cook until bubbly. Adjust texture as desired with additional cooking liquid from the beans, more water or oil. Add salt, if needed, and pepper to taste.

1 28-OUNCE CAN ITALIAN TOMATOES,
WITH JUICE

1 CUP ONION, FINELY CHOPPED

2 TABLESPOONS FRESH JALAPEÑO
PEPPER, SEEDED AND FINELY
CHOPPED, OR TO TASTE

3 CLOVES GARLIC, FINELY CHOPPED

½ TEASPOON SALT OR TO TASTE

1 TO 2 TEASPOONS SUGAR OR PURE
MAPLE SYRUP OR TO TASTE

1 8-OUNCE CAN TOMATO SAUCE

makes about 4 cups

MI CASA SALSA

This is a killer sauce for fajitas, for dipping tortilla chips,
or for any food that screams for a touch of salsa.

Place tomatoes in food processor and pulse on and off to finely chop. In a saucepan, combine tomatoes with onion, pepper, garlic, salt, sugar or syrup, and tomato sauce over medium heat. Bring to a boil, lower heat and simmer for 30 minutes or until slightly thickened. Adjust seasoning with salt and sugar, if needed. Cook about 5 minutes longer.

Cool then refrigerate up to 2 weeks. Serve cool or at room temperature. Use for fajitas or as a sauce for dipping tortilla chips.

Tip: For a less chunky sauce,
add onion, pepper and garlic to food processor.
Pulse on and off several times to more finely chop
ingredients. Do not puree.

BEING A NATIVE *Texan,*

FIFTH GENERATION AT THAT,

cowboy WAYS ARE IN MY BLOOD.

I LIKE TO HARKEN BACK

TO THE DISHES I WAS *raised on.*

PART OF THE CURRENT

popularity IS THAT THE GENERAL

PUBLIC IS SAVVY ENOUGH TO SPEND

GOOD MONEY FOR *this kind*

OF FOOD. THE PUBLIC HAS GROWN

BEYOND TYPICAL

cowboys AND *Indians.*

—Stephan Pyles
founder of the Star Canyon restaurants,
Dallas and Las Vegas

PICO DE GALLO

This fresh salsa is great for shrimp,
beef, or chicken fajitas.

Combine tomatoes, pepper, onion and garlic in a medium bowl. Toss to combine. Add salt, mixing well. Allow to stand about 1 hour. Add cilantro, mixing gently. Serve with fajitas.

4 RIPE TOMATOES
(ABOUT 2 CUPS COARSELY CHOPPED)

2 FRESH SERRANO PEPPERS, SEEDED
AND FINELY CHOPPED,
OR TO TASTE

½ CUP ONION, COARSELY CHOPPED

2 CLOVES GARLIC, FINELY CHOPPED

1 TEASPOON SALT OR TO TASTE

½ CUP CHOPPED FRESH CILANTRO,
LOOSELY PACKED

makes 2¹/₂ to 3 cups

GUACAMOLE

Mashed avocado dip is required for fajitas.
Guacamole is also a wonderful dip for tortilla chips or
as a garnish for just about any grilled beef, chicken,
pork, fish, or wild game.

Peel avocados and place pulp in a medium bowl. Use a fork or potato masher to coarsely mash. Add tomato, onion, salt, and lemon or lime juice. Stir and mash again to desired consistency. Mixture should not be too smooth. Serve immediately with fajitas or as a dip for tortilla chips.

2 LARGE RIPE AVOCADOS OR ENOUGH TO
MAKE ABOUT 2 CUPS

1 SMALL TOMATO, SEEDED AND FINELY
CHOPPED

1 TABLESPOON FINELY CHOPPED OR
GRATED ONION, DRAINED

½ TEASPOON SALT OR TO TASTE

1 TO 2 TABLESPOONS LIME OR LEMON
JUICE OR TO TASTE

makes 2¹/₂ cups

I'VE ALWAYS WORN *boots.*

I BOUGHT MY FIRST PAIR OF POINTED

COWBOY BOOTS WHEN I WAS WORKING AT THE

Maisonette, A FRENCH RESTAURANT IN

CINCINNATI, OHIO. THE CHEF LAUGHED AND SAID,

"OKAY, YOU'RE SOME *cowboy* NOW."

AFTER TAKING A JOB IN DALLAS, I COULD TELL

THAT WEARING *boots* HERE WAS THE *norm.*

SO I STARTED WEARING THEM IN THE *kitchen.*

NO ONE COULD BELIEVE

A *chef* IN COWBOY BOOTS.

BUT NOW

I GET THEM

AS PRESENTS.

—*Dean Fearing*
executive chef, The Mansion on Turtle Creek,
Dallas

SOUTHWESTERN HOT FUDGE SUNDAE

At dessert time, there's nothing better than a chocolate sundae. Crisp-fry a flour tortilla shell and fill it with ice cream and hot fudge to make a cowboy happy.

Drape a flour tortilla over a small soup or ice cream bowl. Use that bowl as a frame to shape the tortilla "bowls." In a small skillet, heat 1 inch of oil over medium-high heat. Carefully slide a tortilla into hot oil. When it puffs and begins to turn golden (1 to 3 minutes), remove from heat and drape over the bowl. As it cools, the tortilla will crisp and hold the bowl shape.

When tortilla has cooled enough to hold the shape, invert. Sprinkle inside with cinnamon sugar mixture; set aside. Repeat with remaining tortillas; set aside. Store in airtight containers for 1 to 2 days.

Coarsely chop chocolate. Combine chopped chocolate with cream in a small saucepan. Cook over low heat, stirring constantly, until chocolate is melted. Cool until thickened. Reheat gently to serve warm. May be served cold, as well; store in refrigerator up to 1 week.

To assemble sundaes, place 2 scoops of ice cream in a tortilla "bowl." Pour hot fudge sauce to taste over ice cream. Garnish with chopped pecans, sliced bananas, and a dollop of whipped cream, if desired.

4 FLOUR TORTILLAS

OIL FOR FRYING

4 TABLESPOONS SUGAR PLUS ½ TEASPOON CINNAMON

8 OUNCES SEMISWEET CHOCOLATE

1 CUP HEAVY CREAM

8 SCOOPS VANILLA ICE CREAM

½ CUP CHOPPED PECANS

2 BANANAS, SLICED, OPTIONAL

WHIPPED CREAM, IF DESIRED

Shortcut:
Use bottled fudge sauce. Heat according to label directions.

makes 4 servings

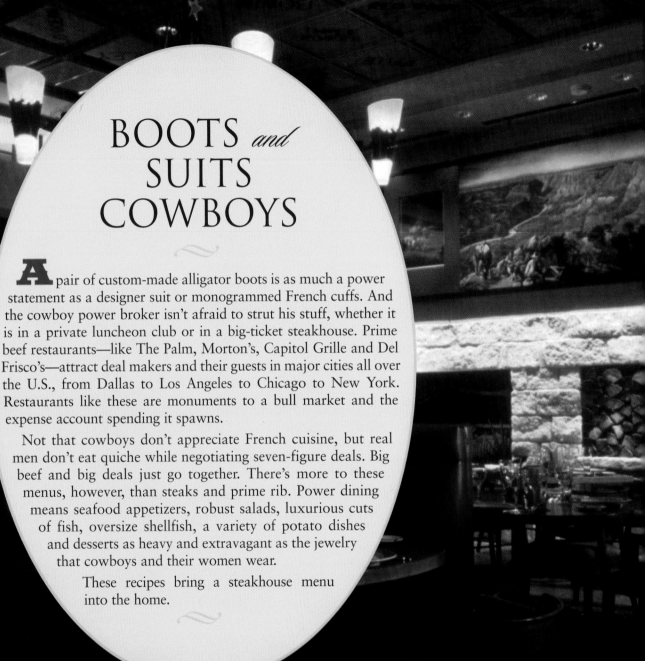

BOOTS *and* SUITS COWBOYS

A pair of custom-made alligator boots is as much a power statement as a designer suit or monogrammed French cuffs. And the cowboy power broker isn't afraid to strut his stuff, whether it is in a private luncheon club or in a big-ticket steakhouse. Prime beef restaurants—like The Palm, Morton's, Capitol Grille and Del Frisco's—attract deal makers and their guests in major cities all over the U.S., from Dallas to Los Angeles to Chicago to New York. Restaurants like these are monuments to a bull market and the expense account spending it spawns.

Not that cowboys don't appreciate French cuisine, but real men don't eat quiche while negotiating seven-figure deals. Big beef and big deals just go together. There's more to these menus, however, than steaks and prime rib. Power dining means seafood appetizers, robust salads, luxurious cuts of fish, oversize shellfish, a variety of potato dishes and desserts as heavy and extravagant as the jewelry that cowboys and their women wear.

These recipes bring a steakhouse menu into the home.

RAW BAR APPETIZER

*Start off a power lunch or dinner with an example
of nature's Viagra—oysters on the half shell.
Always good to have a little extra aggression when
negotiating a multimillion dollar deal at noon.*

Arrange 4 (each) oysters and clams in a shallow bed of ice on 4 well-chilled plates. Serve immediately with Mignonette Sauce and Cocktail Sauce.

16 (EACH) OYSTERS AND CLAMS ON
   THE HALF SHELL
MIGNONETTE SAUCE
COCKTAIL SAUCE

MIGNONETTE SAUCE

2 TO 3 TABLESPOONS LEMON JUICE

1 CUP CHAMPAGNE VINEGAR

¼ CUP FINELY CHOPPED SHALLOTS

1 TEASPOON SALT OR TO TASTE

1 TEASPOON PEPPER OR TO TASTE

In a small bowl, combine lemon juice, champagne vinegar, shallots, salt and pepper to taste, stirring well. Serve in small ramekins for dipping or place about 1 teaspoon of one of the sauces on each oyster on the half shell.

makes about 1 cup

Tip: For a really sumptuous raw bar, also offer jumbo boiled shrimp and giant crab claws.

COCKTAIL SAUCE

1 CUP KETCHUP

1 CUP CHILI SAUCE

2 TABLESPOONS LEMON JUICE OR TO TASTE

2 TEASPOONS PREPARED HORSERADISH OR TO TASTE

1 TO 2 TEASPOONS WORCESTERSHIRE SAUCE OR TO TASTE

1 TO 2 DROPS RED PEPPER SAUCE OR TO TASTE

In a small bowl, combine ketchup, chili sauce, lemon juice, horseradish, Worcestershire sauce, and red pepper sauce in a small bowl. Blend well. Refrigerate 1 hour before serving. Serve in small ramekins for dipping.

makes about 2 cups

makes 4 servings

LOBSTER BISQUE

Lobster bisque has become standard on steakhouse menus because those same restaurants serve a bunch of lobster, too. Bisque is a great way to use up shells and lobsters that may not be big and bold enough to appear solo on a table. It's also very good.

1 LIVE LOBSTER (1½- TO 2½-POUND) OR 2 TO 3 FROZEN LOBSTER TAILS

1 SMALL ONION, CUT IN HALF

1 LARGE CARROT, CUT IN 4 PIECES

1 LARGE RIB CELERY, CUT IN 4 PIECES

¼ CUP OLIVE OIL

4 CUPS WATER

1 CUP HALF-AND-HALF

1 TABLESPOON ALL-PURPOSE FLOUR

1 TABLESPOON BUTTER, SOFTENED TO ROOM TEMPERATURE

½ TEASPOON SALT OR TO TASTE

½ TEASPOON WHITE PEPPER OR TO TASTE

⅓ CUP DRY SHERRY OR TO TASTE

Shortcut:
Have lobster steamed at fish market or seafood counter of supermarket. Remove meat from shell and claws; set aside. Roast shells with vegetables as above. Chop lobster meat and use instead of roast lobster.

makes 4 to 6 servings

Grip live lobster with a towel or pot holder on a cutting board. Using the tip of a large, sharp knife, pierce the head of the lobster at the point on its back where the head joins the tail. Thrust the knife point through the shell to the board to kill the lobster quickly and painlessly. If using frozen lobster tails, thaw and proceed as with whole lobster.

Preheat oven to 425°. Place lobster or lobster tails in a large, shallow roasting pan, meaty side up. Using a knife tip, cut from the head or head end through the abdomen covering so the tail meat is exposed. Break the shell if necessary so it will lie flat.

Arrange onion, carrot and celery around the lobster. Drizzle vegetables and lobster with olive oil. Place pan in oven and roast, stirring vegetables several times, until the lobster is cooked through and meat is snowy white, about 20 minutes for whole lobster, 10 to 12 minutes for tails. Do not overcook.

Remove lobster or lobster tails from roasting pan. Allow to cool enough to handle. Crack the claws and remove the meat; chop coarsely and set aside. Slip a knife between the tail and the shell to loosen tail meat; chop coarsely and set aside. Set aside all shells and lobster head.

Meanwhile, return vegetables to oven and roast until well-browned and fork-tender, 10 to 20 minutes longer. Remove roasting pan from oven and place on one or two burners of stovetop. Add head and shells to the pan, along with water. Bring liquid to a boil over high heat. Lower to simmer and cook for 30 to 45 minutes or until liquid is reduced to about 2½ to 3 cups, stirring occasionally to loosen any morsels stuck to the pan.

When liquid is reduced, remove vegetables and lobster shells from pan. Strain liquid through a double thickness of cheesecloth into a clean saucepan. Place pan over low heat.

Stir in half-and-half. Blend flour and butter to form a smooth paste. Using a whisk, stir butter-flour mixture into soup. Stir and cook until thickened. Add salt and white pepper to taste. Add chopped lobster meat and heat through but do not boil. Add sherry just before serving.

CRAB CAKES

In the '90s, crab cakes were a spark of magic on most restaurant menus. And they're still a favorite, especially in the hallowed halls where "boots and suits" cowboys dine.

Pick over crab to remove any shell or cartilage; set aside. In a medium bowl, stir together mayonnaise, mustard, and eggs, mixing well. Gently stir in crab, ⅓ cup breadcrumbs, parsley, red pepper sauce, salt and black pepper. Divide mixture into 12 round cakes, about ½-inch thick. Roll crab cakes in remaining bread crumbs, gently pressing crumbs into all sides.

Heat ½ inch vegetable oil in a large skillet over medium heat until very hot, almost smoking. Carefully place crab cakes into hot oil. Do not crowd pan, sides should not touch. Cook for 2 to 4 minutes on each side or until golden brown. Cook crab cakes in batches, adding more oil as needed. Serve with a dollop of Remoulade Sauce.

1 POUND FRESH LUMP CRABMEAT

2 TABLESPOONS MAYONNAISE

2 TABLESPOONS DIJON MUSTARD

2 EGGS, LIGHTLY BEATEN

1⅓ CUP FRESH BREADCRUMBS, DIVIDED USE

2 TABLESPOONS CHOPPED FRESH PARSLEY

2 TO 3 DROPS RED PEPPER SAUCE TO TASTE

½ TEASPOON SALT OR TO TASTE

½ TEASPOON BLACK PEPPER OR TO TASTE

ABOUT ½ CUP VEGETABLE OIL, ADDITIONAL AS NEEDED

REMOULADE SAUCE

REMOULADE SAUCE

1½ CUPS MAYONNAISE

4 TEASPOONS DIJON MUSTARD

1 ANCHOVY, MASHED, OR 1 TEASPOON ANCHOVY PASTE

2 TABLESPOONS FINELY CHOPPED PARSLEY

2 TABLESPOONS CAPERS, DRAINED AND CHOPPED

1 TEASPOON DRIED CHERVIL

1 TO 2 TEASPOONS LEMON JUICE OR TO TASTE

In a small bowl, combine mayonnaise, mustard, anchovy, parsley, capers, chervil, and lemon juice to taste. Blend well and refrigerate at least 1 hour.

makes 6 servings,
2 crab cakes per serving

In the *beginning*—when none of us knew what we were doing—

we were just trying to *break free* from the rigid structure

of *French cuisine.* I was looking more to Mexican techniques

and a rustic image. There wasn't a lot of *cowboy cuisine* to draw from.

Cowboy cooking was part of cowboys just trying to stay alive.

So were we in the early '80s. I tried to stay close to *local products*

and close to the *earth* to create something that reflected the freedom,

the individualism, the *rugged* and *primal* connections

that are part of Texas and cowboys. Just as you don't see cowboys

in *aristocratic* outfits, we didn't make our food according to the

European traditions. We didn't *strain* our *sauces.*

—Robert Del Grande
chef-owner of Cafe Annie,
Houston

CHOP CHOP GREEK SALAD

Cowboys enjoy salad when there's something to it besides delicate leafy greens. This salad has plenty to chew on.

Peel cucumber. Cut in half lengthwise and scrape out seeds. Cut into bite-size pieces; set aside.

Cut tomatoes in half and gently squeeze, cut-side down, to release as many seeds as possible; discard seeds. Cut tomato into bite-size pieces and place in large bowl. Sprinkle tomatoes lightly with ½ teaspoon salt and sugar, tossing to coat evenly. Set aside about 10 minutes.

Add lettuce, onion and cucumber, tossing to combine. Whisk together lemon juice, olive oil, oregano, ½ teaspoon salt and ½ teaspoon black pepper or to taste. Pour over salad and toss to distribute ingredients and evenly coat with dressing. Divide salad among 4 chilled salad plates. Scatter crumbled feta, capers, and olives over salad. Garnish each with an anchovy, if desired. Serve immediately.

1 CUCUMBER

2 LARGE TOMATOES

1 TEASPOON SALT (DIVIDED USE) OR TO TASTE

½ TEASPOON SUGAR

1 12-OUNCE BAG AMERICAN (OR YOUR FAVORITE) SALAD BLEND

½ TO 1 CUP THINLY SLICED RINGS OF RED ONION OR TO TASTE

¼ CUP LEMON JUICE

½ CUP EXTRA-VIRGIN OLIVE OIL

2 TEASPOONS DRIED LEAF OREGANO

3 OUNCES FETA CHEESE (DRAINED WEIGHT), CRUMBLED

2 TABLESPOONS CAPERS, RINSED AND DRAINED, OPTIONAL

12 CALAMATA (GREEK BLACK) OLIVES

4 ANCHOVIES, OPTIONAL

makes 4 servings

6 6- TO 8-OUNCE TROUT FILLETS, SKIN ON

1 CUP FLOUR

1 TEASPOON SALT OR TO TASTE

1 TEASPOON PEPPER OR TO TASTE

4 TABLESPOONS BUTTER, DIVIDED USE

2 TABLESPOONS VEGETABLE OIL

1 TO 1½ CUPS COARSELY CHOPPED PECANS

1 FRESH LEMON

CHOPPED FRESH PARSLEY

PAN-SAUTÉED TROUT FILLETS *with* PECAN BROWN BUTTER

Simple trout fillets are delectable in Houston's or Denver's Petroleum Club or cooked in a skillet over a campfire.

Rinse fillets and shake off excess water; pat dry. Combine flour, salt and pepper, mixing well. Coat all sides of fish lightly with seasoned flour; set aside.

In a large skillet or saute pan, heat 2 tablespoons butter and 2 tablespoons vegetable oil over medium-high heat. Cook fillets 1 or 2 at a time, flesh-side down. Cook 2 to 3 minutes or until edges are golden. Turn and cook another 1 to 2 minutes or until fish flakes easily. Keep warm on a heated plate while preparing the rest of the fillets. If needed, add small amounts of equal parts butter and oil during the cooking.

When all fillets have been cooked, add 2 tablespoons butter to the pan and cook until butter begins to turn golden and gives off a nutty aroma. Add pecans, stirring well, and cook another 1 to 2 minutes until butter is quite brown.

Off heat, stir in a generous squeeze of lemon juice. Add additional salt and pepper to taste, if needed. Pour sauce over fillets and serve immediately. Sprinkle with fresh parsley.

makes 6 servings

SALMON
with MUSTARD CRUST

Cowboys who won't eat fish usually like salmon.
Rich and meaty, salmon passes muster for most
dedicated meat eaters.

Preheat oven to 400°. Spray a shallow baking dish with cooking spray. Rinse and dry fish fillets. Season on all sides with salt and pepper to taste.

In a small bowl, combine mayonnaise and mustard. Spread a thin layer on top of each fillet. Combine breadcrumbs and Parmesan cheese and carefully press a layer of crumbs on top of fish. Arrange fillets in prepared baking dish. Drizzle with lemon juice.

Place in oven and bake for 10 to 12 minutes or until salmon is medium rare to medium. Do not overcook. Cook approximately 10 minutes per inch of thickness at the thickest part.

4 6-OUNCE SALMON FILLETS

½ TEASPOON SALT OR TO TASTE

¼ TEASPOON PEPPER OR TO TASTE

¼ CUP MAYONNAISE

¼ CUP DIJON MUSTARD

1 CUP DRY BREADCRUMBS

1 TABLESPOON GRATED PARMESAN CHEESE

2 TEASPOONS LEMON JUICE

makes 4 servings

THE TRUE BEEF LOVERS—THE GUYS WHO CAN *afford* IT—KNOW WHO'S GOT THE BEST STEAK IN TOWN. THEY'VE CHANGED FROM *six guns* TO *16-ounces* OF MEAT. THEY LOVE THE GOOD THINGS IN LIFE AND THEY'RE WILLING TO SPEND THEIR *money* ON IT. WHEN I FIRST GOT INTO THE STEAKHOUSE BUSINESS IN THE '80S, THERE WAS A LOT OF *free-flowing money.* IT'S EVEN BIGGER NOW BECAUSE THEY GO FOR THE *wines.* THESE GUYS USED TO KNOW NOTHING ABOUT WINES. BUT TODAY THEY DO, AND THEY'RE WILLING TO *spend* TO GET WHAT THEY WANT.

—Dale Wamstad
founder of III Forks and Del Frisco's steakhouses,
Dallas

DAILY SEAFOOD
SPECIAL
with TEQUILA SALSA

*This sauce works with just about any fish—from red snapper
to redfish to swordfish to halibut to seabass to salmon.
So take your pick; grill it or broil it.*

Rinse and dry fillets and shrimp; set aside.

Preheat broiler. Place chilies in a flat pan or heat-proof skillet and position about 6 inches under heat. Broil until blistered and charred on all sides, turning occasionally, about 6 to 10 minutes. Place chilies in a plastic bag and seal to steam and soften chilies.

Allow chilies to cool. Remove from bag, peel skin under running water. Remove seeds and ribs. Coarsely chop roasted chilies.

In a saucepan over medium heat, cook onions and garlic in 2 tablespoons olive oil until onions wilt and begin to soften. Add roasted peppers. Stir in tequila and allow liquid to boil. Remove pan from heat and set aside.

Preheat broiler or prepare coals for grilling. Allow coals to burn down until covered with gray ash. Lightly paint fillets and shrimp with remaining olive oil. Season generously with salt and pepper.

Broil or grill just until shrimp turn snowy white and fish firms, about 1 to 2 minutes on each side for shrimp; 2 to 4 minutes per side for fish, depending on thickness.

Lightly brush with olive oil after turning and season generously with salt and pepper. Remove from grill and brush the remaining side with olive oil. Keep warm.

Return saucepan to low heat, stir in lime juice, salt and pepper to taste. Add tomatoes and cook, stirring occasionally, 1 to 2 minutes or until sauce heats through. For a thicker, richer sauce, whisk in butter, 1 tablespoon at a time. Remove from heat.

Garnish each fillet with 2 shrimp and a small dollop of sauce.

4 6-OUNCE RED SNAPPER OR OTHER FISH
FILLETS

8 JUMBO SHRIMP, PEELED WITH
TAILS ON

2 MEDIUM ANAHEIM OR NEW MEXICO
GREEN CHILIES OR 1 8-OUNCE CAN
CHOPPED GREEN CHILIES, DRAINED

1 CUP CHOPPED ONION

2 CLOVES GARLIC, FINELY CHOPPED

3 TABLESPOONS OLIVE OIL, DIVIDED USE

1½ OUNCES GOLD TEQUILA

1 TEASPOON SALT OR TO TASTE

1 TEASPOON PEPPER OR TO TASTE

1 TABLESPOON LIME JUICE OR TO TASTE

1 LARGE TOMATO, SEEDED AND CHOPPED

3 TABLESPOONS BUTTER

makes 4 servings

BONE-IN RIBEYE *with* FRIED ONION STRINGS

1 10- TO 12-OUNCE BONE-IN BEEF
RIBEYE STEAK PER PERSON

1 CLOVE GARLIC PER STEAK

2 TABLESPOONS OLIVE OIL PER STEAK

¼ TEASPOON SALT (OR FAVORITE
SEASONING BLEND) PER STEAK,
OR TO TASTE

¼ TEASPOON PEPPER PER STEAK,
OR TO TASTE

1 TABLESPOON UNSALTED BUTTER
PER STEAK, OPTIONAL

FRIED ONION STRINGS (SEE
FOLLOWING RECIPE)

makes 1 serving

Prime beef is hard to find outside a steakhouse. If you're a really good customer, you might be able to buy some steaks from your favorite cow palace. Even if you can't get prime beef, a top grade of choice—like Certified Black Angus Beef cut to your specifications by a butcher—will do just fine. Grill the steaks over hot coals or in a cast-iron skillet over direct heat. The oven broiler just doesn't get hot enough. Those in steakhouses hit 1,500° and higher to achieve the dark exterior finish with the red interior. Hot coals or a skillet heated to smoking are your best bet.

Have butcher cut steaks about 1½ to 2 inches thick. Rinse and dry steaks and place in a single layer in a shallow pan. Finely chop garlic and combine with olive oil. Pour over steaks, turning to make sure steaks are well-coated with olive oil. Spoon some of the garlic on top and press into the steaks, turn and press garlic into other sides as well.

Allow steaks to marinate at room temperature for about an hour. Meanwhile, prepare fire if grilling over coals. Coals are ready when they burn a bright red-orange. Spread coals so that there is a very hot side of the grill and a somewhat cooler area. This allows you to control the heat under the meat.

If using a cast-iron skillet, place skillet over low heat about 5 minutes before cooking to allow pan to heat through. A couple of minutes before cooking, raise heat to high. The pan should begin to smoke.

When ready to cook steaks, remove steaks from oil, shaking off garlic and excess oil. Season generously on both sides with salt and pepper. Place on grill or in hot pan. Cook 3 to 6 minutes or as needed to leave char marks on the meat. Turn and char other sides.

Depending on the thickness of the meat and the cooking temperature, the steaks may be almost to the desired degree of doneness. If the meat seems to

be getting too dark or is burning, remove to a slightly cooler area of the grill or lower heat under skillet. Cook 4 to 6 minutes longer or as desired.

Medium rare—warm, red center—is recommended, although some cowboys like theirs rare with a cool, red center. Medium is a pink center and no good steak should ever suffer the indignity of being cooked any more than that.

To test for medium rare without piercing the meat to glimpse the color, press the center of the steak. If it feels and appears the same consistency as the ball of the hand—the fleshy part right under the thumb—it is medium rare.

Keep warm until serving time and serve on heated plates as soon as possible. Just before serving, place 1 tablespoon butter on each steak to melt. Garnish with a handful of Fried Onion Strings.

FRIED ONION STRINGS

Soaking the onion rings in buttermilk or milk makes the
flour stick. For a heavier batter, use buttermilk.
Want a thin batter? Use milk.

1 LARGE SWEET ONION

1 CUP BUTTERMILK OR MILK

1 CUP FLOUR

1 TEASPOON SALT OR TO TASTE

1 TEASPOON BLACK PEPPER OR TO TASTE

¼ TEASPOON CAYENNE PEPPER OR
   TO TASTE

1 PINT VEGETABLE OIL

Slice onion into thinnest rings possible. Place onion rings in a shallow dish. Pour buttermilk or milk over onions, cover and refrigerate at least 1 hour. In a plastic bag, combine flour, salt, black and cayenne peppers. Shake to evenly distribute ingredients.

Heat oil to 375° in a deep saucepan or deep fryer. Remove a small handful of onion rings from buttermilk, shaking off excess. Drop onion rings into flour, separate rings, and shake to coat.

Drop a few rings at a time into hot oil and cook until golden. Remove from hot oil with a slotted spoon and drain on a paper towel. Repeat with remaining rings until all rings have been battered and fried. Keep warm.

makes 4 servings

DENVER
LAMB CHOPS

*These lamb chops reflect the culinary traditions
of sheep raisers, many descended from Basque and
Greek shepherds, who settled in the Western states.
After steak, even cattle raisers often swear by
a big, juicy lamb chop.*

Rinse and dry lamb chops. Place in a single layer in flat pan; set aside, covered and refrigerated. Whisk together garlic, sage and olive oil. Allow to steep 30 minutes to 1 hour. Remove lamb chops from refrigerator. Pour olive oil marinade over lamb chops, turning in the marinade to coat all surfaces evenly. Cover loosely and allow to come to room temperature while preparing grill.

Arrange enough coals to cover the bottom of the grill. Arrange in a mound and light coals. When coals are burning, spread evenly over the bottom of the grill. Allow to burn down until coals are beginning to turn gray but still glowing. Coals should be hot. Test temperature by holding hands no more than 4 to 5 seconds at cooking level.

When coals are ready, remove chops from marinade, allowing excess to drain off. Season liberally on both sides with salt and pepper. Grill on both sides, about 2 to 3 minutes per side, or until medium rare or to desired degree of doneness, preferably no more than medium. Remove lamb chops to a warm platter. If desired, brush lightly with melted butter.

12 DOUBLE-CUT LAMB CHOPS

2 CLOVES GARLIC, CRUSHED

1 TABLESPOON CRUMBLED, NOT GROUND, SAGE LEAVES

½ CUP EXTRA-VIRGIN OLIVE OIL

SALT TO TASTE

PEPPER TO TASTE

¼ CUP BUTTER, MELTED (OPTIONAL)

makes 4
(3 chops per person) to
6 (2 chops per person)
servings

1 8- TO 10-OUNCE THICK VEAL CHOP PER
PERSON

2 TABLESPOONS OLIVE OIL PER
VEAL CHOP

1 3- TO 4-INCH SPRIG FRESH ROSEMARY
OR 1 TEASPOON DRIED PER VEAL CHOP

½ TEASPOON SALT OR TO TASTE PER
VEAL CHOP

½ TEASPOON PEPPER OR TO TASTE PER
VEAL CHOP

ROQUEFORT BUTTER (SEE PAGE 117)

*Tip: For additional
flavor, deglaze the skillet
with equal parts water and port,
about ¼ cup each. Cook over medium
heat until liquid is reduced by at least
half, scraping up any bits that may be
stuck to the pan. Strain and serve
as pan juices with veal chop and
Roquefort Butter.*

makes 1 serving

VEAL CHOP
with ROSEMARY

*Good veal can be almost as hard to find as prime beef.
Again, if you have access to a wholesale supplier—
or a prime steakhouse friend—who will sell you some
of these top quality cuts, count yourself lucky and
shell out what it takes.*

Rinse and dry veal chops. Place in a single layer in a shallow pan. In a measuring cup, whisk together olive oil and rosemary. If using fresh rosemary, pull rosemary leaves from the stem. Pour rosemary olive oil over veal, turning veal to coat all sides well. Spoon some of the rosemary on top. Cover and marinate at room temperature for 1 hour.

Preheat a cast-iron or other heavy-bottom skillet over high heat until quite hot, but not smoking. Remove veal chop from olive oil, shaking off excess. Season to taste with salt and pepper.

Take skillet off heat and carefully place chop in skillet. Return to heat and reduce to medium high. Cook 2 to 3 minutes or until edges are seared and brown; turn and sear the other side, 2 to 3 minutes.

Lower heat to medium and cook 3 to 4 minutes longer, depending on desired degree of doneness and thickness of the meat. Veal is best served medium with a pink center. The center of the veal should be slightly less yielding to the touch than the ball of the hand, the fleshy part underneath the thumb.

Remove veal and keep warm until ready to serve. Serve as soon as possible on a hot plate with a slice of Roquefort Butter melting on top.

ROQUEFORT BUTTER

This also goes well with beef or pork.

In a small bowl, blend butter, Roquefort, white vermouth, shallots and parsley to make a smooth spread. Using wax paper or plastic wrap, shape butter mixture into a log shape, about 1 inch in diameter, and refrigerate until firm. Cut in ¼-inch rounds. Wrap and refrigerate (1 week or less) or freeze (1 month or less) any left over.

6 TABLESPOONS UNSALTED BUTTER, SOFTENED AT ROOM TEMPERATURE

4 TABLESPOONS ROQUEFORT (OR OTHER BLUE) CHEESE, SOFTENED AT ROOM TEMPERATURE

1 TEASPOON WHITE VERMOUTH

½ TEASPOON VERY FINELY MINCED SHALLOTS

¼ CUP MINCED PARSLEY

makes 8 servings

4 CHICKEN QUARTERS OR AIRLINE
  BREASTS (BONED HALF BREAST WITH
  DRUMMETTE ATTACHED), SKIN ON

3 TABLESPOONS BALSAMIC VINEGAR

2 TABLESPOONS LEMON JUICE

½ CUP EXTRA-VIRGIN OLIVE OIL

¼ CUP PURE MAPLE SYRUP

1 TO 2 TABLESPOONS WHOLE BLACK
  PEPPERCORNS, COARSELY CRUSHED

1 TO 2 TEASPOONS SALT, OR TO TASTE

1 TO 2 TABLESPOONS COARSELY GROUND
  BLACK PEPPER

makes 4 servings

MAHOGANY FIRE-ROASTED CHICKEN

The "airline" chicken breast is a popular restaurant cut because it is white meat and easy to eat but still has the heft and flavor of meat on the bone.

Rinse and dry chicken. Purchase chicken halves or create your own airline bird by deboning the breast portion of a breast quarters. Run the tip of a knife between the bone and the breast meat, being careful not to separate the breast meat from the wing. Press the breast meat to flatten it. Use poultry shears to snip off the wing tip, leaving a boneless chicken breast attached to a wing drummette.

Place chicken in 1 or 2 large, resealable plastic bags and add vinegar, lemon juice, oil, maple syrup, and black peppercorns. Turn bag several times to mix marinade ingredients and evenly coat the chicken. Marinate at room temperature for 1 hour. For longer marination, refrigerate chicken.

Preheat oven to 450°. Position shelf in the middle of the oven. Remove chicken from marinade, allowing excess to drip back into the bag. Season chicken with salt to taste. Set aside marinade.

Arrange chicken skin side up in a single layer in a large, flat baking pan. Place in preheated oven for 15 minutes for chicken quarters, 10 minutes for "airline" breasts. Baste chicken with some reserved marinade and reduce oven temperature to 375°.

Roast chicken quarters another 30 to 35 minutes; "airline" breasts about 20 to 25 minutes. Test for doneness by piercing the thick part of the breast near the wing joint. Juices should run clear.

Additional basting, if desired, will add several more minutes to cooking time. Adjust accordingly. If desired, crisp the skin a bit more by placing chicken under the broiler for up to 2 to 3 minutes. Be careful not to burn skin.

GOURMET GREEN BEANS

Vegetable side dishes are often served family-style in steakhouses. This is a wonderful way to enjoy green beans, with a steak or any other entree.

In medium saucepan, cook frozen green beans according to package directions until beans are easily pierced with a fork, tender, but not mushy. Drain beans and rinse with cold water to stop cooking. In medium saucepan, melt butter over medium high heat. When butter begins to bubble, add shallots, grated lemon rind, salt and pepper to taste. Add beans to saucepan, toss to coat evenly and heat through. Season to taste with salt and pepper.

1 16-OUNCE PACKAGE FROZEN PREMIUM QUALITY WHOLE GREEN BEANS

3 TABLESPOONS UNSALTED BUTTER

1 TABLESPOON FINELY CHOPPED SHALLOT

1 TABLESPOON GRATED LEMON RIND (YELLOW PART ONLY)

1 TEASPOON SALT OR TO TASTE

½ TEASPOON PEPPER OR TO TASTE

makes 6 to 8 servings

CREAMED SPINACH

Confirmed spinach haters have learned to like this green leafy vegetable when served steakhouse-style with lots of garlic and cream sauce.

Place fresh spinach in a sink full of cold water. Drain and rinse sink to wash away any sand particles. Refill sink and allow about 5 minutes for any other debris to sink to the bottom of the sink.

Carefully remove spinach leaves to a colander, pulling off stems and discarding any discolored leaves. Don't try to shake off all the water. Place spinach leaves in a large saucepan over medium heat. Cover and cook until spinach wilts, about 5 minutes. Drain spinach and set aside.

If using frozen spinach, cook according to package directions. Drain spinach in a colander and press with the back of a spoon to remove excess liquid. In a medium saucepan, combine butter, shallots and garlic over medium heat. Cook until shallots are soft, about 3 minutes. Do not brown butter or garlic. Stir in cream cheese and stir to melt. Add sour cream, spinach, salt and nutmeg, mixing well. Heat through, but do not boil.

2 BUNCHES FRESH SPINACH OR 2 10-OUNCE PACKAGES FROZEN WHOLE LEAF SPINACH

2 TABLESPOONS BUTTER

¼ CUP FINELY CHOPPED SHALLOTS OR ONION

2 CLOVES GARLIC, FINELY CHOPPED

1 3-OUNCE PACKAGE CREAM CHEESE, CUBED

½ CUP SOUR CREAM

½ TEASPOON SALT OR TO TASTE

¼ TEASPOON GRATED NUTMEG

makes 4 to 6 servings

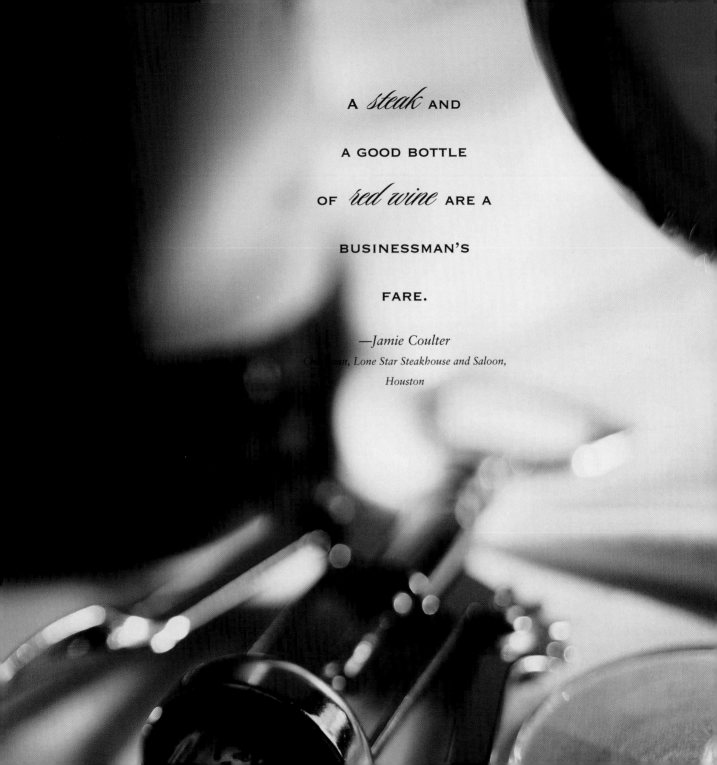

A *steak* AND

A GOOD BOTTLE

OF *red wine* ARE A

BUSINESSMAN'S

FARE.

—*Jamie Coulter*
Chairman, Lone Star Steakhouse and Saloon,
Houston

SMASHED ROASTED GARLIC POTATOES

Everybody loves potatoes, especially when they're redolent with garlic. Cowboys are no exception. These are wonderful with any grilled meat or fish.

Preheat oven to 400°. Separate garlic into individual cloves. Place in an ovenproof skillet or small baking dish. Pour olive oil over garlic. Place in oven for 30 minutes or until garlic cloves are soft. Remove and allow to cool enough to handle. Squeeze pointed end of cloves to release roasted garlic from the peel. Trim root end if necessary. Mash enough roasted garlic to make 1 tablespoon or to taste. Refrigerate any remaining roasted garlic coated with a thin layer of olive oil for up to 1 week.

Scrub potatoes, cutting larger ones into sizes roughly equal to the smaller potatoes. Place in a large saucepan with enough water to cover. Add salt. Place potatoes over high heat until water boils. Reduce heat slightly and cook potatoes for 15 to 20 minutes or until potatoes may be easily pierced with a fork.

Drain potatoes, reserving about ½ cup of the cooking liquid. Return potatoes to the saucepan and mash coarsely, using a potato masher or the back of a fork. Add some of the cooking liquid if potatoes seem dry. Stir in 2 to 3 tablespoons olive oil or a combination of butter and olive oil and mashed roast garlic. Adjust seasoning to taste with salt and pepper.

1 HEAD GARLIC

¼ CUP PLUS 2 TO 3 TABLESPOONS GOOD QUALITY EXTRA-VIRGIN OLIVE OIL, DIVIDED USE

2 TO 2½ POUNDS YUKON GOLD OR NEW RED POTATOES

WATER

1 TABLESPOON SALT OR TO TASTE

½ TEASPOON PEPPER OR TO TASTE

makes 4 to 6 servings

1 QUART BUTTERMILK

¾ CUP SUGAR

2 CUPS HEAVY CREAM

2 TEASPOONS VANILLA

BOTTLED CARAMEL SAUCE OR
HOMEMADE CAJETA
(MEXICAN-STYLE CARAMEL SAUCE)

1 PINT FRESH RASPBERRIES,
BLUEBERRIES, BLACKBERRIES OR
STRAWBERRIES (OR A COMBINATION)

FRESH MINT

makes 10 to 12 servings

¾ CUP SUGAR, DIVIDED USE

2 CUPS MILK OR GOAT'S MILK,
DIVIDED USE

1 TEASPOON CORNSTARCH DISSOLVED IN
2 TEASPOONS WATER

⅛ TEASPOON BAKING SODA

makes 8 servings

BUTTERMILK ICE CREAM *with* FRESH BERRIES *and* CAJETA

Just forget that cowboys don't drink buttermilk. They'll love the sweet-tart flavor of this rich homemade ice cream, especially with fresh berries and Cajeta—a rich Mexican caramel sauce.

In a large mixing bowl, combine buttermilk, sugar, cream and vanilla. With electric beaters at low speed, beat until sugar is dissolved, 3 to 5 minutes. Pour into freezer container of an ice cream machine. Process according to manufacturer's instructions or until mixture stiffens, about 10 to 15 minutes. Pack additional ice around container and allow ice cream to season at least an hour.

Serve 2 scoops in a puddle of caramel sauce or homemade Cajeta. Garnish with plenty of fresh berries and mint leaves.

CAJETA
(MEXICAN CARAMEL SAUCE)

True Cajeta is made with goat's milk for an even deeper, richer flavor with a tart bite. But cow's milk will do, although canned goat's milk has become more available in healthfood stores and in some supermarkets.

In a large saucepan over medium heat, stir sugar until it melts. Cook until golden brown, or a caramel color. Remove from heat.

Pour ½ cup milk in a small bowl and stir in cornstarch and baking soda; set aside.

Place remaining 1½ cups milk in a medium saucepan over medium heat and bring just to the boiling point. Return caramelized sugar to low heat. Slowly add hot milk to caramelized sugar, stirring constantly. Stir in reserved milk mixture.

Cook, stirring occasionally, for up to 1 hour. After about 40 minutes, sauce will begin to thicken and require more frequent stirring to prevent sticking. Cajeta is ready when it is quite thick and golden in color.

6 OUNCES BITTERSWEET CHOCOLATE

6 TABLESPOONS UNSALTED BUTTER

¼ CUP COCOA

½ TEASPOON VANILLA

4 EGG WHITES, AT ROOM TEMPERATURE

⅛ TEASPOON CREAM OF TARTAR

2 TABLESPOONS GRANULATED SUGAR

CONFECTIONERS' SUGAR

MINT LEAVES, OPTIONAL

FRESH RASPBERRIES OR
STRAWBERRIES, OPTIONAL

CAJETA SAUCE, OPTIONAL
(SEE PAGE 122)

HEAVY CREAM, OPTIONAL

VANILLA ICE CREAM, OPTIONAL

*Tip: Prepare batter
ahead of time and refrigerate,
as long as overnight, until about
30 minutes before baking.*

makes 8 servings

CHOCOLATE LAVA

*This dessert has been adopted by restaurants from
coast to coast. Also known as molten chocolate,
these individual pudding cakes are wonderful alone,
with a simple sprinkling of confectioners' sugar,
a mint leaf and fresh berries. Or, splurge the cowboy way,
with a puddle of Cajeta, a drizzle of cream or a big scoop
of vanilla ice cream—and the confectioners' sugar,
the mint leaf and the berries.*

Preheat oven to 400°. Coat 8 individual pudding tins or large muffin cups lightly with butter and a sprinkling of sugar. Shake out excess.

In a large microwave safe bowl, combine chocolate and butter. Microwave on high for 60 seconds; stir. Microwave on high for 30 seconds longer, as needed, stirring each time until chocolate and butter are melted and smooth.

Sift in cocoa. Add vanilla and stir until smooth; set aside. Place egg whites and cream of tartar in a medium bowl. Use electric beaters, beat until soft peaks form. Gradually add sugar and continue beating until stiff peaks form.

Fold about ¼ of the chocolate mixture into the egg whites, being careful not to deflate. Then fold egg white mixture into the chocolate. Fill muffin cups about three-quarters full. Bake until cakes are cracked on top but still gooey in the middle, about 7 to 8 minutes. Let sit for 2 to 3 minutes. Invert to unmold onto wax paper.

Serve hot. Garnish with a sprinkling of confectioners' sugar, a mint leaf and fresh berries. If desired, serve on a puddle of Cajeta or caramel sauce, drizzled with a stream of heavy cream; or serve with vanilla ice cream.

A *steakhouse* IS AN ARENA—
IT'S FIGHT NIGHT.
THAT'S WHAT'S HAPPENING
DURING AN *expense account* DINNER
OVER BUSINESS *negotiations* AND
confrontations.

—Gene Street
*Owner, Cool River steakhouse and
president of Consolidated Restaurant Cos. Inc.,
Dallas*

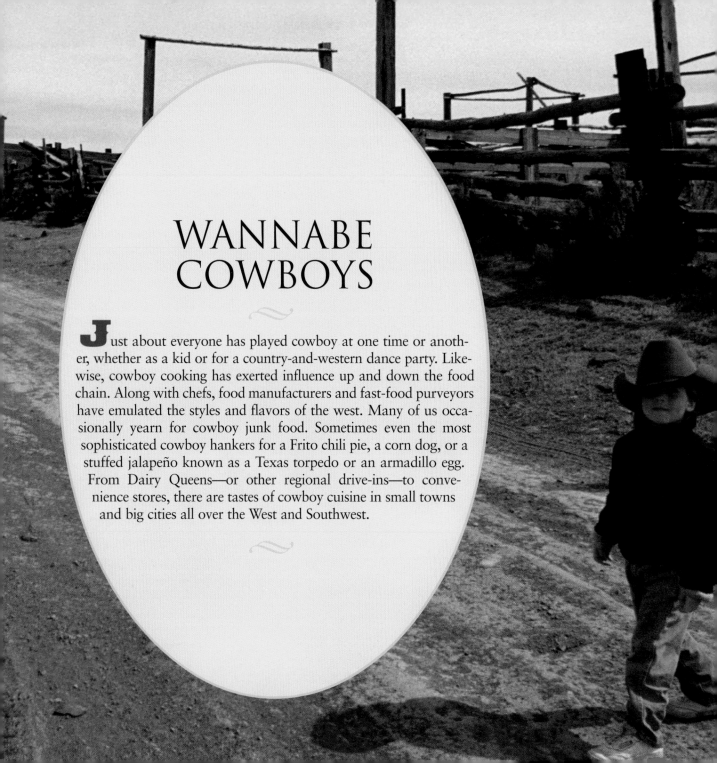

WANNABE COWBOYS

Just about everyone has played cowboy at one time or another, whether as a kid or for a country-and-western dance party. Likewise, cowboy cooking has exerted influence up and down the food chain. Along with chefs, food manufacturers and fast-food purveyors have emulated the styles and flavors of the west. Many of us occasionally yearn for cowboy junk food. Sometimes even the most sophisticated cowboy hankers for a Frito chili pie, a corn dog, or a stuffed jalapeño known as a Texas torpedo or an armadillo egg. From Dairy Queens—or other regional drive-ins—to convenience stores, there are tastes of cowboy cuisine in small towns and big cities all over the West and Southwest.

"CHILI" CON QUESO

*Homemade chile con queso (literally cheese with chile peppers)
can be delicate and quite divine. This junk food version,
however, is substantial and easy to make.
Great for tortilla-chip dipping or ladling over some tamales.*

Combine chili and picante in a large, microwave-safe bowl. Cut cheese into 2-inch chunks and stir into chili mixture. Microwave on high for 60 seconds. Stir and microwave 60 to 30 seconds at a time until cheese is melted and mixture is hot and bubbly.

*Tip: Combine all ingredients
in a crock pot about 1 hour before the party.
Heat on high, stirring occasionally. When all the
ingredients are melted, reduce heat to low and
serve out of the crockpot to keep the
cheese bubbling hot.*

2 CUPS CHUCK WAGON CHILI (SEE PAGE 3) OR 1 19-OUNCE CAN CHILI

½ CUP MI CASA SALSA (SEE PAGE 96) OR USE BOTTLED SALSA

2 POUNDS PROCESS AMERICAN CHEESE SUCH AS VELVEETA

makes 10 to 12 servings

FRITO CHILI PIE

*Of course, you could make this with tortilla chips
or another brand of corn chip. But the folks who
make Fritos made this dish famous with their suggestion
to ladle chili over chips in the bag and eat them that way.
It remains a cowboy's favorite quick fix.*

In a small saucepan or microwave safe bowl, heat chili until bubbly. Place chips in a large soup bowl or on a plate (or slit the side of a small package) and ladle chili over the chips. Garnish with chopped onions, if you don't plan on kissing your horse that afternoon, and cheese.

1 10-OUNCE CAN CHILI

1 10-OUNCE PACKAGE FRITO CORN CHIPS

1 TABLESPOON CHOPPED ONIONS, OPTIONAL

¼ CUP GRATED YELLOW CHEESE

makes 1 serving

ABOUT 2 CUPS FROZEN FRENCH FRIES,
HEATED OR FRIED ACCORDING TO
PACKAGE INSTRUCTIONS

1 8-OUNCE CAN CHILI OR
1 CUP CHUCK WAGON CHILI (SEE
PAGE 3), HEATED

½ CUP GRATED CHEDDAR CHEESE

SLICED JALAPEÑOS, CRUMBLED BACON,
CHOPPED ONIONS FOR GARNISH,
OPTIONAL

BOTTLED RANCH DRESSING FOR
DIPPING, OPTIONAL

makes 1 serving

2 DOZEN CANNED OR
BOTTLED WHOLE JALAPEÑO PEPPERS

1 CUP YELLOW CORNMEAL

1 CUP FLOUR, DIVIDED USE

½ TEASPOON SALT

1 TABLESPOON VEGETABLE OIL

1 CUP MILK

3 CUPS VEGETABLE OIL OR
AS NEEDED FOR FRYING

3 TO 4 OUNCES YELLOW OR
MONTEREY JACK CHEESE

makes 24 peppers

CHILI CHEESE FRIES

*Messy, sure. Also incredibly filling and tasty.
Think chili on fries with melted cheese. Admit it.
You want some now.*

Preheat oven to 400°. Place french fries on an ovenproof plate. Top with chili and cheese. Place in oven just until cheese melts, about 3 minutes. Garnish as desired, with jalapeños, bacon, and onions. Serve with a small bowl of Ranch-style dressing for dipping french fries. You'll need a fork.

TEXAS TORPEDOES
(FRIED JALAPEÑOS)

*Buying these frozen and simply dropping them in
hot oil is a lot easier but not nearly as rewarding.
Some junk food just begs to be tried homemade.*

Rinse and dry peppers to remove the packing oil or brine. Make a small slit in each pepper. Carefully remove seeds and membranes, being careful not to tear the pepper. Rinse inside of peppers and drain well.

In a small bowl, combine cornmeal, ½ cup flour and salt. Add 1 tablespoon oil and milk, mixing until smooth. Allow batter to rest for 10 to 15 minutes. Cut cheese into small pieces and stuff each pepper with cheese. Roll each pepper in ½ cup flour, then dip in batter to cover. Refrigerate at least 30 minutes.

Place enough oil in a small saucepan or deep fryer to come up about 3 inches. Heat to 350°. Fry peppers a few at a time in hot oil 1 to 2 minutes or until golden brown. Drain on paper towels and keep warm. Repeat until all peppers are battered and fried. Serve immediately.

CHILI MAC

Freshly cooked with enough of a spice jolt to give it flavor,
this easy skillet meal can be pretty darn good.
Ask a cowboy, just learning to cook.

In a large skillet over medium-high heat, crumble ground beef. Stir to break up lumps and cook until all pink disappears. Pour off excess grease.

Stir in chili powder, cumin, garlic, salt and pepper to taste, stirring to coat meat. Add tomatoes and their liquid, as well as tomato sauce. Bring liquid to a boil, lower heat to simmer and cook uncovered, stirring occasionally, for 15 to 20 minutes or until sauce is thickened and no longer soupy. Fold in macaroni. Garnish each serving with shredded cheese.

STEAK FINGER BASKET

Nothing says cowboy finger food any more
eloquently than this favorite,
which is a staple in many small-town restaurants.

Prepare beef strips according to package directions or follow recipe for Chicken-Fried Steak. Keep beef strips warm. Prepare Cream Gravy, according to recipe and keep warm.

Heat french fries according to package directions for deep-frying or baking in the oven. Serve immediately with gravy on the side for dipping.

1 POUND LEAN GROUND BEEF

1 TABLESPOON CHILI POWDER

1 TEASPOON GROUND CUMIN

1 TEASPOON GRANULATED GARLIC

1 TEASPOON SALT OR TO TASTE

1 TEASPOON PEPPER OR TO TASTE

1 16-OUNCE CAN CHOPPED TOMATOES

1 8-OUNCE CAN TOMATO SAUCE

½ PACKAGE (8 OUNCES) MACARONI, COOKED ACCORDING TO PACKAGE DIRECTIONS

8 OUNCES YELLOW CHEESE, GRATED

makes 4 servings

1 POUND FROZEN BATTERED BEEF STRIPS OR CUT BEEF CUBE STEAK INTO STRIPS AND BATTER AND FRY AS FOR CHICKEN-FRIED STEAK

CREAM GRAVY (P. 77)

½ PACKAGE FROZEN FRENCH FRIES

makes 2 servings

1 POUND LEAN GROUND BEEF

1 MEDIUM ONION, CHOPPED
   (ABOUT 1 CUP)

1 8-OUNCE CAN TOMATOES, UNDRAINED

1 4-OUNCE CAN GREEN CHILIES,
   DRAINED

1 TEASPOON GRANULATED GARLIC

2 TEASPOONS SALT OR TO TASTE,
   DIVIDED USE

1 TEASPOON PEPPER OR TO TASTE

1 TABLESPOON CHILI POWDER

1½ CUPS YELLOW CORNMEAL OR
    MASA HARINA

3 CUPS WATER, DIVIDED USE

1 TABLESPOON MELTED BUTTER

makes 4 to 6 servings

TAMALE PIE

*Not quite as simple as Chili Mac, this one-pot meal also
has great flavor. Frozen versions are available,
but never quite as good as the real thing—homemade.*

Preheat oven to 350°. Grease bottom of a 9-inch square baking dish. In a large skillet over medium-high heat, crumble ground beef. Stir to break up lumps and cook until almost all pink disappears. Stir in onion and continue cooking until onion is soft and beef begins to brown.

Add tomatoes, using the back of a spoon to crush and break them into pieces. Stir in green chilies, garlic, 1 teaspoon salt, pepper and chili powder. Bring liquid to a boil, reduce heat and cook uncovered 15 to 20 minutes, stirring occasionally.

Meanwhile, slowly add cornmeal or masa harina and 1 teaspoon salt to 1 cup cold water in a saucepan. Heat remaining 2 cups water to boiling and gradually stir into cornmeal or masa. Place cornmeal or masa over medium heat; cook and stir about 5 minutes or until batter begins to sputter. Remove from heat.

Spoon half the cornmeal or masa batter in an even layer in the bottom of the baking dish. Fill with meat sauce. Cover filling with remaining cornmeal or masa batter, smoothing the top. Brush lightly with melted butter. Bake for 20 to 30 minutes or until brown on top.

PEOPLE TELL ME I'M THE ONLY *Harvard-educated* COWBOY

THEY KNOW. BUT I WAS RAISED AROUND RANCHING AND MANY

DAYS I'D RATHER BE *building fence* THAN PRACTICING LAW,

BUT I DO LOVE PRACTICING LAW, TOO. TWICE A YEAR WE

GATHER UP THE CALVES TO SELL AND WORK THE CATTLE.

WHEN WE'RE *branding* AND *working* CATTLE, WE SOMETIMES

HAVE SOME "NON-WORKING" COWBOYS COME OUT TO HELP.

THERE ARE A LOT OF *wannabe cowboys* AROUND—

GUYS FROM *bank presidents* TO *university professors*

WHO HAVE A HORSE AND JUST ENJOY BEING AROUND A RANCH.

YOU MIGHT SAY RANCHING IS MY GOLF GAME.

—*Glenn Floyd*
Lawyer and rancher,
Norman, Oklahoma

DINER HASH BROWNS
and SCRAMBLED EGGS
with CHEESE

This is a typical Big Breakfast a la diners
and roadside coffee shops all over the country—
just perfect when you feel the need
for late night sustenance after an evening
of boot scootin'.

In a large skillet over medium-high heat, cook bacon until crisp. Drain on paper towels, crumble and set aside. Drain all but 2 tablespoons bacon drippings.

In a medium bowl, toss together potatoes, onion and parsley. Return skillet to low heat. When oil is hot, add potato mixture and spread evenly in the pan. Season with ¼ teaspoon each salt and pepper or to taste. Cover and cook until potatoes are golden brown and crusty. Turn in one piece, if possible. This is easier to do if you slide potato mixture out of skillet onto a plate, crisp-side down. Using a spatula, invert plate and potatoes and ease potatoes into skillet.

Cook, uncovered, until potatoes begin to brown and crisp on other side. Combine eggs, water, ¼ teaspoon each salt and pepper or to taste. Pour eggs evenly over potato mixture. Lower heat and cook until eggs are set, about 4 to 5 minutes. Slide onto plate and sprinkle top with cheese and crumbled bacon. Cut in wedges to serve.

4 SLICES BACON

4 CUPS FROZEN SHREDDED HASH BROWN POTATOES

2 TABLESPOONS SLICED GREEN ONION, WHITE PART ONLY

1 TABLESPOON CHOPPED PARSLEY

½ TEASPOON SALT OR TO TASTE, DIVIDED USE

½ TEASPOON PEPPER OR TO TASTE, DIVIDED USE

4 EGGS, WELL-BEATEN

4 TABLESPOONS MILK OR WATER

½ CUP GRATED CHEDDAR CHEESE

makes 2 to 4 servings

1 ⅓-POUND GROUND BEEF PATTY

½ TEASPOON SALT OR TO TASTE,
    DIVIDED USE

½ TEASPOON PEPPER OR TO TASTE,
    DIVIDED USE

½ CUP THINLY SLICED ONION RINGS

2 SLICES RYE, WHITE OR WHEAT BREAD

1 TABLESPOON BUTTER OR MARGARINE

1 SLICE SWISS CHEESE

PATTY MELT
with GRILLED ONIONS

*This is another staple of many fast-food and
roadside-grill menus. Like the eggs, this short-order
recipe is highly recommended after a tequila sunrise.*

Heat a small skillet or griddle over medium-high heat. Season both sides of ground beef with ¼ teaspoon each salt and pepper or to taste. Cook hamburger on one side until brown, 3 to 4 minutes. Turn and cook until brown on other side, 3 to 4 minutes longer. Cook beef to medium, with very little pink in the middle.

Remove ground beef and keep warm. Add onions and season with ¼ teaspoon each salt and pepper or to taste. Stir onions into beef patty drippings. Cook until tender and brown at the edges. Remove and keep warm.

Wipe out skillet or griddle and place over medium heat. Spread 1 side of each slice of bread with butter or margarine. Place beef patty on dry side of 1 bread slice, spread beef with onions, then top onions with cheese. Add second bread slice, butter-side up. Place buttered sandwich in skillet or on griddle and cook until bread toasts on one side, about 3 minutes. It should be golden brown. Turn and toast other side.

Slice diagonally and serve immediately.

makes 1 serving

EVERYBODY WHO VACATIONS IN *Colorado* THINKS

THEY HAVE TO BUY A *cowboy hat*. AND THEY TELL

ONE OF THE THREE GREAT LIES:

"I'VE *always* WORN COWBOY BOOTS."

YOU CAN ALWAYS TELL A *Rexall ranger*

(A DRUGSTORE COWBOY). THEY DON'T LOOK

TOO *dirty* AND THEY DRIVE A RANGE ROVER.

—Greg Abernathy
Breckenridge, Colorado

3 CUPS FLOUR

1 TEASPOON SALT

1 CUP CHILLED VEGETABLE SHORTENING
  OR LARD

1 EGG

1 16-OUNCE CAN CHOCOLATE PIE
  FILLING

3 CUPS VEGETABLE OIL OR AS NEEDED

makes 18 pies

CHOCOLATE FRIED PIES

Few desserts are as difficult to find these days as good fried pies,
especially the chocolate variety—so try them yourself.
Prepared chocolate pie filling is recommended in this recipe
because the commercial texture stands up to the frying process.
A homemade mixture, however, might disintegrate.

Combine flour and salt in a mixing bowl or in the work bowl of a food processor. Using a pastry blender (or the on-off pulse of a blender), cut in shortening or lard until the mixture resembles coarse crumbs.

Lightly beat egg in a measuring cup. Add enough cold water to make ¾ cup. Make a well in the flour mixture and add egg mixture. Stir with a fork until the dough comes together. If using a food processor, add egg mixture and process until dough forms a ball. Wrap dough in plastic wrap and chill for at least 30 minutes.

Divide dough and shape into balls about 2 inches in diameter. Roll out each ball between sheets of wax paper into a 5-inch circle. Spoon about 2 teaspoons filling onto half of each circle, leaving a 1-inch border.

Moisten edges of pastry with water, fold edges over to form a half circle. Press edges together with a fork dipped in flour. Repeat with remaining dough to make about 18 pies. Chill pies at least 30 minutes before frying.

Add vegetable oil to a depth of 1½ inches in a heavy skillet or deep fryer. Heat to 375°. Fry pies a few at a time. Do not crowd fryer. Fry for 2 to 3 minutes per side until golden brown. Drain on paper towel, using additional towels to blot the top. Fry remaining pies as above.

DRIED FRUIT FILLING *for* FRIED PIES

For a variation, fill pastry with a fruit filling.

Place dried fruit in a saucepan and add enough water to cover. Soak overnight. Put saucepan over medium high heat and bring liquid to a boil. Reduce heat to low and simmer fruit, uncovered, for 30 minutes or until soft. Stir occasionally and mash fruit with the back of a spoon.

Add sugar as needed depending on the sweetness of the fruit—more for apricots, a bit less for apples. Stir in nutmeg, cinnamon for apples, salt, butter and lemon juice. To thicken, stir in dissolved cornstarch and cook 2 to 3 minutes longer. Mixture should be thick like jam. Cool before filling pastry as above.

2 CUPS DRIED APRICOTS OR APPLES

2 CUPS WATER OR AS NEEDED

1 TO 1½ CUPS SUGAR

¼ TEASPOON GRATED NUTMEG

¼ TEASPOON CINNAMON,
    IF USING APPLES

¼ TEASPOON SALT

¼ CUP BUTTER

1 TO 2 TEASPOONS LEMON JUICE

3 TABLESPOONS CORNSTARCH
    DISSOLVED IN 3 TABLESPOONS WATER

SHORTCUT: USE PREPARED JAM.

makes 3 cups

BLACK TIE
and BOOTS
COWBOYS

When President George W. Bush was inaugurated, party invitations read "black tie and boots." In Texas and other states with cowboy etiquette—this isn't unusual. For men, that generally means a tuxedo shirt and jacket, jeans with a starch crease, a black-felt Stetson, and custom-made boots. For women, it may mean designer dresses or lots of butter-soft leather, fringe, silver turquoise jewelry, and custom-made boots. Short of formal but much more dressed up than casual, this style of entertaining has its own brand of cuisine—as well as attire.

The following "black tie and boots" parties feature complicated menus, as well as simple barbecues.

When the YO Ranch celebrated its centennial on April 12, 1980, with the first of the parties that would come to be known as the YO Social Club, I was just back in the office as a Food Editor for *The Dallas Morning News*. After six weeks maternity leave, I was determined to cover the event. So, with new baby at my breast, I headed for the Texas Hill Country, expecting a glorious spring outing along wild-flower-lined roads.

Known for fierce storms and changing weather, the Hill Country (just west of San Antonio) is also one of the most beautiful areas in the world with live oaks, rugged limestone cliffs and rivers that can rage and trickle in the same day. After a beautiful four-hour drive, the weather turned as sharply as my car as I headed down the ranch road. By evening, snow—big, blanketing flakes—was falling.

That first party will always be remembered as "the night it snowed," since winters here often come and go without any snow, much less in April. But it takes more than bad weather to bring a halt to anything on the YO. The snow didn't stick and the party went on, as it has almost every year since.

YO RANCH SOCIAL CLUB

The YO is one of Texas' legendary ranches. Descendants of Capt. Charles Schreiner still continue operations on the spread that lists Mountain Home, Texas, as its mailing address. Besides cattle, the Shreiners are also pioneers in raising exotic game—black buck antelope, axis deer, nilgai antelope—on the rugged territory within their wide-ranging fences. They also operate a summer camp, as well as a year-round dude ranch and a conference center.

The annual YO Ranch birthday party is the ultimate "black tie and boots" occasion. Friends from all over the world descend on the Texas Hill Country to celebrate the cowboy tradition that lives on at the YO.

The menu is always upscale Texas ranch cuisine, often using meat from the animals raised on the ranch. Ostrich fajitas, wild boar tacos, and nilgai antelope rib chops are likely to be served from any of the several food kiosks set up in the outdoor dining pavilion, patio, and game room on the ranch.

Because of the strong German influence in this part of the state, the menu usually reflects the multicultural influences of European settlers, indigenous native Americans (the Comanches ruled this part of the state), Spanish conquerors, and Mexican nationals. Inevitably the menu is pick-up casual. And no Texas party is complete, of course, without Margaritas and Shiner Bock beer.

The following buffet menu is designed for a similar black-tie-and-boots event—fancy but fun.

Menu

REAL DEAL MARGARITAS

AVOCADOS STUFFED WITH GULF OF MEXICO BLUE CRAB

GAME SAUSAGE WITH POTATOES

ANTICHUCHOS

VENISON SAUERBRATEN WITH BISCUITS AND HORSERADISH CREAM

GORDITAS WITH HILL COUNTRY CABRITO OR WILD TURKEY MOLE

PRALINES

ANEJO ALEJANDRO

REAL DEAL MARGARITAS

Make the Southwest's favorite cocktail by the pitcher to keep a big party rolling.

In a large pitcher, combine lime juice and sugar, stirring to dissolve sugar. Add tequila, Triple Sec, and ice cubes. Stir until well-chilled. If desired, place salt around the rim of the glass. Moisten edges of small cocktail tumblers, Margarita or martini glasses. Dip rims in salt to coat. Strain Margarita cocktail into salt-rimmed glass over ice or straight up. Serve immediately. Garnish, if desired, with thin slice of lime.

5 CUPS FRESH LIME JUICE OR LIME JUICE FROM FROZEN CONCENTRATE (NOT MARGARITA MIX OR LIMEADE), CHILLED

1⅓ CUPS SUGAR

5 CUPS TEQUILA (BUY THE GOOD STUFF—YOU'LL FEEL BETTER IN THE MORNING), CHILLED

⅓ CUP TRIPLE SEC (ORANGE LIQUEUR)

ICE CUBES

COARSE BAR SALT

THIN SLICES OF LIME

makes 10 cocktails

AVOCADOS STUFFED *with* GULF OF MEXICO BLUE CRAB

This can be made for cocktail party fare—as a stand-up appetizer—or served at a sit-down dinner. Take your pick— either way, the tastes are unforgettable.

Pick over crab to remove any pieces of shell or cartilage. In a small bowl, combine crabmeat, mayonnaise, sour cream, salt and pepper to taste. Use just enough mayonnaise and sour cream to moisten the crab, but not so much as to drown the delicate taste and texture. Adjust sea-

1 POUND LUMP CRAB MEAT (PREFERABLY FROM TEXAS GULF COAST BLUE CRABS)

2 TABLESPOONS MAYONNAISE

2 TABLESPOONS SOUR CREAM

¼ TEASPOON SALT OR TO TASTE

¼ TEASPOON PEPPER OR TO TASTE

2 TO 3 DROPS RED PEPPER SAUCE OR
   TO TASTE

6 SMALL, RIPE (BUT NOT TOO SOFT)
   AVOCADOS

JUICE FROM 2 LEMONS OR AS NEEDED

WORCESTERSHIRE SAUCE

GARNISHES: FINELY CHOPPED TOMATO,
FINELY CHOPPED GREEN ONION,
RED AND BLACK CAVIAR (USE VERY
SMALL ROE), LIME WEDGES

CAYENNE PEPPER (OPTIONAL)

makes 12 hors d'oeuvres or
appetizer servings;
6 entree salad servings

soning with a few drops of red pepper sauce. Refrigerate until ready to stuff avocado halves.

Since avocados tend to darken with exposure to air, cut and stuff avocados as close to serving time as possible. Holding an avocado in one hand, run the tip of a sharp knife around the center, horizontally, to cut through the skin and the meat of the avocado. A tough round seed in the middle prevents the knife from going all the way through.

To separate halves of avocado, use both hands to twist top and bottom in opposite directions, like unscrewing the top of a mayonnaise jar. The seed will remain in one of the halves. Using a sharp, heavy-bladed knife, smack the seed with the knife blade so it sticks. Twist the knife to "unscrew" the seed. Discard seed.

For "walk-around" hors d'oeuvre, do not peel avocados. To serve as a first (or main) course, carefully remove peel. Use a spoon to separate peel from the avocado flesh. Remove the avocado half from the peel in one piece.

Drizzle or paint all exposed surfaces—outside, too, if using peeled avocados—of each half with lemon juice. Place a couple of drops of Worcestershire sauce in the seed cavity, then fill with a generous dollop of crab salad.

Garnish with a sprinkling of finely chopped tomato, onion, red and black caviar. Again brush exposed surface of avocado with lemon juice. If desired, dust cut edge of avocado very lightly with cayenne pepper for an additional touch of color and for flavor zing. Season lightly because cayenne packs quite a punch.

If storage before service is required, cover with plastic wrap and refrigerate no longer than 1 hour. Serve immediately, if possible.

To serve stuffed avocado halves as "walk-around" hors d'oeuvres: stuff unpeeled avocados and serve with salad forks for digging out the avocado and crab filling. No plates are needed; the peel serves as an au naturel cocktail plate for eating out of hand. Offer lime wedges.

To serve on plates as an appetizer course (or as a main dish salad): place 1 or 2 stuffed avocado halves on a salad or luncheon plate lined with salad greens. Place 1 or 2 lime wedges on each plate.

12 SMALL RED NEW POTATOES

1 TEASPOON SALT OR TO TASTE

1 POUND WILD GAME OR OTHER
FULL-FLAVORED SAUSAGE

1 TABLESPOON OLIVE OR VEGETABLE OIL
OR AS NEEDED

1 RED BELL PEPPER

1 GREEN BELL PEPPER

1 LARGE ONION

1 TEASPOON PEPPER OR TO TASTE

12 OR MORE FLOUR TORTILLAS (SEE
PAGE 45), HEATED

MI CASA SALSA (SEE PAGE 96)

FRESH CILANTRO LEAVES

makes 12 hors d'oeuvres or
appetizer servings;
4 to 6 entree servings

GAME SAUSAGE
with POTATOES

Venison, duck, or pheasant sausage makes this a
YO Ranch-style treat, but almost any link sausage will do.
Beef, pork or turkey Polish sausages also work well.
Lamb sausage is divine. This is a great dish to prepare on
the grill outdoors using a wok or a gas-powered wok.

In a large saucepan over high heat, place potatoes in enough cold water to cover. Add 1 teaspoon salt or to taste. Bring water to a boil. Lower heat slightly, cover and cook until potatoes are tender, easily pierced with a fork about 12 to 15 minutes. Drain and cool completely. This may be done a day or two ahead.

Cut sausage into ½-inch slices. If potatoes are small enough (about 1 inch), leave whole, otherwise cut in half or into quarters, depending on size. Cut off tops of peppers and remove seeds and membranes. Cut into 1-inch pieces. Cut off root end of onion, peel and cut into 1-inch pieces.

Assemble all ingredients for stir-frying. Heat a large skillet or wok over medium-high heat (stove top, coals, or gas-powered grill). Add sausage and cook until brown, about 5 minutes. Remove sausage and reserve.

Add oil and heat through. Stir in potatoes and cook, stirring occasionally, until potatoes begin to brown, about 5 minutes. Add onions. When onions begin to wilt and soften, add red and green peppers. Stir and cook until peppers are shiny with oil and just begin to soften. Season to taste with salt and pepper. Keep warm.

Wrap tortillas in foil and place in 300° oven for 20 minutes or until heated through. For "walk-around" hors d'oeuvres buffet service, spoon some of the sausage and potato filling from the grill wok into warm flour tortillas. Allow guests to garnish as desired with salsa and cilantro.

To serve at table, divide sausage and potatoes among flour tortillas. Roll around filling and stack on serving plate or dinner plates, seam side down. Keep warm. Offer picante sauce and cilantro leaves as garnish. Also makes a good Mexican-style breakfast entree.

ANTICHUCHOS

*This traditional appetizer, popular in
San Antonio and South Texas, is fun to eat on a stick—
or be polite and cut the meat from the skewer and
eat it with a fork.*

In a large resealable plastic bag, combine oil, vinegar, soy sauce, garlic, cumin and chilies. Seal bag and shake to mix well. Rinse and dry meat and drop into bag with marinade. Seal bag and shake well to evenly coat beef or venison. Refrigerate for 4 hours up to overnight. Soak skewers in water at least 1 hour before grilling.

Remove meat from marinade and set aside. Thread chunks of meat onto skewers, 3 to 4 pieces per skewer. Prepare fire. When coals are glowing red and beginning to cover with gray ash, brush meat with reserved marinade. Season to taste with salt, pepper and a light sprinkling of cayenne.

Grill over hot coals, about 2 to 3 minutes per side, or until meat is medium rare to medium. The center should still be pink. Squeeze lime juice over meat after removing from fire; keep warm.

For "walk-around" hors d'oeuvres, serve on skewers. To serve at table for appetizers or as an entree, serve on skewers with warm flour tortillas and pico de gallo. Strip meat from skewers and wrap in tortillas with pico de gallo, or as desired.

May also be served as an entree with Mexican rice, refried beans, and guacamole on the side.

¾ CUP EXTRA-VIRGIN OLIVE OR VEGETABLE OIL

¼ CUP PINEAPPLE JUICE

3 TABLESPOONS SOY SAUCE

2 TO 3 CLOVES GARLIC, CRUSHED

2 TEASPOONS GROUND CUMIN

2 SERRANO CHILIES, SEEDED AND CUT IN HALF

2½ POUNDS BEEF SIRLOIN OR VENISON, CUT IN 2-INCH CUBES

10 WOODEN SKEWERS

1 TEASPOON SALT OR TO TASTE

1 TEASPOON PEPPER OR TO TASTE

¼ TEASPOON CAYENNE PEPPER OR TO TASTE

2 TO 3 LIMES, CUT IN HALF

10 OR MORE FLOUR TORTILLAS (SEE PAGE 45), HEATED, OPTIONAL

PICO DE GALLO (SEE PAGE 99), OPTIONAL

makes 10 hors d'oeuvres or
appetizer servings;
5 entree servings

OUR *Centennial Celebration* (APRIL 12, 1980) WAS THE BIGGEST,

WILDEST, MOST EXCITING EVENT. I CAME UP WITH THE DRESS CODE

"*black tie* AND *boots.*" I THINK THIS WAS THE FIRST TIME IT HAD EVER BEEN

USED. I SHOULD HAVE COPYRIGHTED IT. TICKETS WERE *free,* BUT SCALPERS

IN KERRVILLE WERE CHARGING BETWEEN *$500* AND *$5,000* PER TICKET.

WE EXPECTED *1,000* GUESTS WHICH WOULD HAVE BEEN LOW BUT FOR A

FREAK APRIL COLD SNAP AND *snowstorm.* THE NEXT WEEK, AN OLD-TIMER SAID

HE REMEMBERED HIS DAD TALKING ABOUT A FREAK SNOWSTORM IN APRIL, 1880

(THE YEAR THE *YO Ranch* WAS FOUNDED). WE HAD SO MUCH FUN,

WE THOUGHT IT'D BE A GOOD IDEA TO PUT ON ANOTHER *party.* WE CALLED IT

THE *YO Social Club* AND WE'VE HAD ONE EVERY YEAR SINCE 1982.

—*Charles Schreiner IV*
YO Ranch,
Mountain Home, Texas

VENISON SAUERBRATEN
with BISCUITS

*This dish reflects the strong German culinary influence
in the Texas Hill Country.*

Rinse and dry meat. Place in a large bowl or nonreactive roasting pan. In a small bowl, stir together mustard and water. Spread evenly over meat and let stand for 10 minutes.

In a saucepan, combine bay leaves, peppercorns, salt, sage, garlic, onion, sugar, stock, vinegar, and bacon drippings or butter. Bring to a boil over high heat. Remove from heat and cool slightly, then pour over meat and allow to cool completely. Cover and refrigerate for 24 to 48 hours, turning occasionally. If the meat will fit in a large, resealable plastic bag, meat may soak in that.

When ready to cook, preheat oven to 250°. Drain marinade from meat; set aside. Dry meat with paper towel. Heat a Dutch oven over medium heat. Spray pan with cooking spray and cook roast on all sides until well-browned, about 10 to 15 minutes.

Pour marinade over browned roast and cover. Place in oven and cook for 3 to 3½ hours or until meat is tender and easily pierced with a fork. Remove meat to warm serving platter. Strain cooking liquid into a large measuring cup and reserve; note the amount. Discard solids. Wipe out cooking pan and pour liquid back in. For each cup of marinade, gradually stir in 1 tablespoon instant dissolving flour and heat over low heat until thickened. Keep warm.

Slice meat into ⅛-inch slices, about the size of a biscuit. Pour just enough of the thickened pan juices over the meat to moisten.

For "walk-around" hors d'oeuvres: stack a couple of slices on the bottom half of a warm split biscuit or dinner roll. Offer with additional gravy and Horseradish Cream. May be eaten as small sandwich or open-face with a fork.

For a dinner entree, serve sliced sauerbraten with mashed potatoes, noodles or spaetzle. Pass gravy and Horseradish Cream.

HORSERADISH CREAM

In a medium bowl, whip cream until stiff peaks form. Add ½ teaspoon salt while beating. Fold in horseradish and sour cream. Cream will hold in refrigerator, covered, up to 3 hours.

4- TO 5-POUND FRESH VENISON, HAM, DEER, ELK OR ANTELOPE, OR 3- TO 4-POUND BEEF CHUCK TENDER

1 TABLESPOON DRIED MUSTARD

3 TABLESPOONS WATER

2 BAY LEAVES

1 TABLESPOON WHOLE BLACK PEPPERCORNS

1½ TEASPOONS SALT OR TO TASTE, DIVIDED USE

1 TEASPOON GROUND SAGE

3 CLOVES GARLIC, CRUSHED

1 CUP CHOPPED ONION (ABOUT 1 MEDIUM ONION)

3 TABLESPOONS BROWN SUGAR

1 CUP BEEF STOCK

½ CUP RED WINE VINEGAR

2 TABLESPOONS BACON DRIPPINGS OR BUTTER

3 TABLESPOONS INSTANT DISSOLVING FLOUR OR AS NEEDED

1 TEASPOON PEPPER OR TO TASTE

25 TO 30 WARM BISCUITS (SEE PAGE 21) OR BAKERY DINNER ROLLS (WHITE, WHOLE GRAIN, RYE, PUMPERNICKEL OR A COMBINATION), SPLIT

HORSERADISH CREAM:

1 CUP HEAVY CREAM

½ TEASPOON SALT OR TO TASTE

⅓ CUP WELL-DRAINED WHITE HORSERADISH

1 SOUR CREAM

makes about 1⅓ cups cream

2 CUPS MASA HARINA

1¼ CUPS HOT WATER OR CHICKEN STOCK

2 TABLESPOONS LARD OR VEGETABLE
SHORTENING

⅓ CUP FLOUR

½ TEASPOON SALT

1 TEASPOON BAKING POWDER

2 CUPS VEGETABLE OIL OR AS NEEDED

SHREDDED ICEBERG LETTUCE

REFRIED BEANS (SEE PAGE 96) OR
USE CANNED, OPTIONAL

HILL COUNTRY CABRITO (SEE
PAGE 151)

WILD TURKEY MOLE (SEE PAGE 153)

CASERA (MEXICAN GOAT CHEESE) OR
FETA CHEESE, CRUMBLED INTO
SMALL PIECES

makes 24 hors d'oeuvres
servings; 12 appetizer
servings; 8 entree servings

GORDITAS
with HILL COUNTRY CABRITO *or* WILD TURKEY MOLE

Gordita means "little fat one" in Spanish and these thick tortillas make great carriers for all sorts of grilled or barbecued meats and fowl.

In a large mixing bowl, combine masa harina with hot water. Cover and let stand for 30 minutes. Add lard or shortening, flour, salt and baking powder. Mix well. Divide the dough into 12 balls. Halve each to make 24 balls. Arrange on wax paper and cover with plastic wrap or damp towels.

Lightly oil fingers. Place a ball of dough in the palm of one hand. Using other hand, pat dough flat to make round about 3 inches in diameter and ¼-inch thick. Pinch edges of gordita to form a ridge around the edge. This helps contain the juices of the topping.

Repeat to shape remaining dough into gorditas. Cover with plastic wrap to prevent drying. Add enough oil to a large skillet to a depth of about ¼-inch. Heat to about 350°. Using a spatula, carefully slide gorditas into hot oil and cook until golden, about 2 minutes. Do not crowd pan. Sides should not touch. The gorditas should be able to float freely. Turn and cook other side until golden, another 1 to 2 minutes. Remove from oil, drain on paper towel and keep warm.

If desired, spread a teaspoon of refried beans on each gordita and top with a tablespoon of shredded lettuce. Add a dollop of barbecued cabrito or turkey mole. Sprinkle each with a few crumbles of Casera or Feta cheese. Serve warm or at room temperature.

HILL COUNTRY CABRITO

*Spanish goats are a major crop on many Texas ranches,
but they also run wild throughout parts of the state.
Young goat—cabrito—is serious Tex-Mex feast food.*

*Lawyer-rancher R. B. Pool swears by the following technique
for cooking cabrito. Missouri cum Texan though he is,
he wouldn't use any kind of sauce on this but Carolina-style
pork barbecue sauce. It is used like a Texas-style
barbecue mop (basting) sauce in this recipe.*

*An electric roaster appliance works great for this,
but it can be cooked in a deep roasting pan in the oven.*

1 YOUNG (13- TO 16-POUND) GOAT,
CUT IN QUARTERS (HAMS AND
SHOULDERS)*

1 PINT OLIVE OIL

½ CUP FINELY CHOPPED GARLIC

1 TEASPOON SALT OR TO TASTE,
DIVIDED USE

2 TO 3 ONIONS, CUT IN FOUR PIECES
EACH

1 OR 2 12-OUNCE DARK BEERS SUCH AS
SHINER BOCK (A TEXAS BEER)

MOP SAUCE FOR CABRITO (SEE
PAGE 152)

FAVORITE BOTTLED BARBECUE SAUCE
OR LET ME CALL YOU SWEET HOT
BARBECUE SAUCE (SEE PAGE 90)

*MAKE SURE YOU HAVE A SKILLET OR ROASTING PAN
LARGE ENOUGH TO HOLD THE CABRITO. A BUTCHER
CAN CUT THE GOAT PIECES SMALL ENOUGH TO FIT
YOUR SKILLET. TRY TO LEAVE PIECES AS LARGE AS
POSSIBLE.

Preheat oven or large electric roaster to 275°. Rinse and dry cabrito; set aside. Heat olive oil in a roaster or roasting pan over medium heat. Add garlic and ½ teaspoon salt. Cook, stirring frequently, until garlic cloves are dark brown.

Add cabrito pieces in single layer, cooking and turning until well-browned on all sides, about 5 to 10 minutes. Repeat as needed until all pieces are browned. Return all goat pieces to roaster or roasting pan with lid.

Pour Mop Sauce for Cabrito over meat. Arrange onion quarters around cabrito. Add enough beer to pan to almost cover cabrito. Cover and roast for 2½ to 3 hours or until meat is falling-off-the-bone tender. Remove from oven and transfer cabrito to a platter. Transfer cooking liquid from roasting pan to a large saucepan, setting aside about 1 cup. Cook over medium heat until reduced by half to two-thirds, or until thickened and syrupy.

Meanwhile, prepare coals for grilling. When coals are covered with gray ash, place cabrito over coals, brushing frequently with 1 cup reserved liquid from the roasting pan. Grilling time will depend on the size of the pieces. Cook until charred at the edges and crisp on the outside about 10 minutes. During last 3 to 4 minutes of grilling, brush with barbecue sauce or reduced cooking liquid to glaze.

For gorditas, allow cabrito to cool enough to handle. Using fingers or a fork, pull meat from bones and chop or shred. Heat with just enough barbecue sauce or any remaining reduced cooking liquid to moisten meat. Use to dollop on gorditas as above or serve on or off bone with plenty of flour tortillas, refried beans, Mexican rice, guacamole and salsa.

MOP SAUCE *for* CABRITO

Place apple juice in a large saucepan over high heat. Add red pepper flakes. When juice boils, lower heat and simmer for 1 hour. As juice cooks away, add additional as needed to maintain a fairly constant 2-cup level.

Add cider vinegar, brown sugar, red pepper sauce, black pepper and salt. Raise heat and bring liquid to a rolling boil. Remove from heat and allow to cool. This may be made ahead and stored in the refrigerator up to 1 month.

---

1 PINT APPLE JUICE PLUS ADDITIONAL AS NEEDED

1 HEAPING TABLESPOON RED PEPPER FLAKES, OR TO TASTE

1 PINT CIDER VINEGAR

1 HEAPING TABLESPOON BROWN SUGAR

¼ CUP BLACK PEPPER OR TO TASTE

¼ CUP SALT OR TO TASTE

makes about 4 cups

WILD TURKEY MOLE

Didn't get a wild turkey during hunting season?
No problem. Substitute a turkey breast from the supermarket.
Don't let the poundage of wild birds startle you.
Although big, a wild turkey is much leaner—
and bonier—than its meatier, domestic cousins.

Rinse and dry turkey or turkey breast. Place in a large stock pot or Dutch oven with enough water to cover. Add carrot, onion, celery, black peppercorns and salt. Bring liquid to a boil over high heat. Cover, reduce heat and simmer until turkey is tender, about to 2 to 3½ hours.

When turkey is done, remove from cooking liquid, setting aside broth. Allow to cool enough to handle. Pull turkey meat from bones, discarding skin. Use two forks to pull the turkey into thin shreds; set aside.

In a medium saucepan, combine mole sauce, enchilada or tomato sauce, and turkey broth, beginning with ½ cup. Add more as needed to adjust consistency and flavor. Heat to boiling, reduce heat to simmer. Stir in peanut butter, chocolate, and sugar. Cook and stir until chocolate is melted, about 5 minutes. Continue simmering 10 minutes longer. Season with ½ teaspoon salt or to taste. If sauce seems too thick, add just enough water or turkey stock to thin to desired consistency.

Place 4 cups shredded turkey breast in a large saucepan. Pour mole sauce over turkey and heat through. Use to fill gorditas as above or to fill crisp taco shells (heated according to package instructions) or flour tortillas.

Use any leftover turkey as desired. Combine the shredded turkey and the remaining strained turkey stock for a good soup. Add cooked white rice or noodles and vegetables.

1 WHOLE WILD TURKEY
(8 TO 10 POUNDS FOR HENS,
14 TO 16 POUNDS FOR MALES) OR
1 (4- TO 6-POUND) TURKEY BREAST

WATER

1 LARGE CARROT, CUT IN 2-INCH PIECES

1 LARGE ONION, QUARTERED

2 LARGE RIBS CELERY, CUT IN 2-INCH
PIECES, INCLUDING LEAVES

1 TABLESPOON BLACK PEPPERCORNS

2½ TO 3 TEASPOONS SALT OR TO TASTE,
DIVIDED USE

1 8¼-OUNCE JAR MOLE SAUCE

1 8-OUNCE CAN TOMATO OR ENCHILADA
SAUCE

RESERVED TURKEY BROTH, ½ TO 1 CUP

1 TABLESPOON SMOOTH PEANUT BUTTER

1 SQUARE DARK, UNSWEETENED
CHOCOLATE

1 TABLESPOON SUGAR

½ TEASPOON SALT

Tip: Substitute leftover roast turkey. Stew carcass for stock.

makes 24 appetizer servings; or filling for about 12 tacos

1½ CUPS SHELLED PECAN HALVES OR
  BROKEN PECAN PIECES

2 CUPS SUGAR

¾ CUP MILK

½ TEASPOON BAKING SODA

1 TEASPOON VANILLA

1 TEASPOON BUTTER

makes 1 dozen

1 PINT VANILLA ICE CREAM
  (TOP-QUALITY)

¼ CUP ANĚJO TEQUILA (DO NOT
  SUBSTITUTE STANDARD TEQUILA)

1 TABLESPOON TRIPLE SEC OR GRAND
  MARNIER (OR OTHER ORANGE LIQUEUR)

2 TO 3 ICE CUBES

  NUTMEG

makes 3 servings

PRALINES

*Pralines are the ultimate finish to any meal with lots of
Tex-Mex flavors. There's usually a platterful at the cash register
of any truly great Tex-Mex restaurant. So rich, so monstrous,
so chock full of nuts, you wonder why they're the perfect
ending to a meal as big as an Enchilada Special can be.
No one knows why. They just are. And they're great
as a walk-about handheld dessert, as well.*

Place pecans in a large skillet over low heat. Stirring frequently and watching carefully to prevent burning, cook until pecans start to brown and begin to smell toasty. Remove from heat and pour out of pan to stop the cooking; set aside toasted pecans.

In a large saucepan, combine sugar, milk and soda. Cook over high heat, stirring constantly, Bring mixture to a boil. Continue boiling and stirring until it reaches 240° on a candy thermometer (soft ball stage).

Remove from heat and add vanilla, butter and pecans. Using a wooden spoon, beat until mixture begins to hold a shape. Drop by small ice cream scoop onto lightly greased or buttered wax paper, flatten slightly.

ANĚJO ALEJANDRO

*This is a variation on the time-honored Brandy Alexander.
The main difference is that this one uses barrel-aged tequila
called anějo. Try one as a sippable dessert.*

In a blender container, combine ice cream, tequila, Triple Sec and a couple of ice cubes. Blend until smooth. Pour into chilled brandy snifters. Sprinkle each serving lightly with nutmeg.

GLITZ AND GITTER

SCOTTSDALE, ARIZONA

*There's an annual charity event in Scottsdale, Arizona,
called Glitz and Glitter that offers desert cowboys
a grand occasion for black ties and boots.
Ladies go all out in soft leather or crushed
velvet skirts—Western broomstick style,
of course—with lots of Indian-styled turquoise jewelry.
"The glitzier the better," says Charlotte Loudermilk,
a volunteer for the event.*

*A typical sit-down menu at the event held at Reata Pass,
a party ranch, is basic cowboy fare, centering on a grilled steak,
grilled corn, and beans with some Southwestern
touches thrown in.*

Menu

BEEFSTEAK TOMATOES AND MOZZARELLA SALAD
WITH CILANTRO
OK CORRAL T-BONE STEAKS WITH CHILE-LIME BUTTER
COWBOY BAKED BEANS
GRILLED CORN
BANANA PUDDING DE ROTHWELL
SOPAIPILLAS

BEEFSTEAK TOMATOES *and* MOZZARELLA SALAD *with* CILANTRO

4 TO 6 LARGE VINE-RIPE TOMATOES

2 POUNDS FRESH MOZZARELLA

1½ TEASPOONS SALT OR TO TASTE

2 TEASPOONS CRACKED BLACK PEPPER
OR TO TASTE

1 CUP TOP-QUALITY EXTRA-VIRGIN
OLIVE OIL OR TO TASTE

1 CUP CILANTRO LEAVES,
LOOSELY PACKED, COARSELY
CHOPPED

Big vine-ripe tomatoes and mozzarella cheese are a classic combination. Substituting cilantro for the traditional basil gives it a Southwestern touch.

Slice tomatoes ½-inch thick. Slice mozzarella ¼- to ½-inch thick. Arrange slices of tomato and mozzarella alternately on salad plates, lightly salting each slice of tomato. Grind fresh pepper over cheese and tomatoes. Drizzle with olive oil and garnish with a sprinkle of cilantro.

Alternate method: Trim ends of tomatoes and cut tomatoes into 1-inch chunks. Place in a large salad bowl and add salt to taste. Cut cheese into ½-inch chunks. Toss cheese with tomatoes along with black pepper to taste and enough olive oil to coat the ingredients but not so much that the tomatoes rest in a puddle of oil. Sprinkle salad with cilantro leaves. Serve on chilled plates.

makes 8 servings

OK CORRAL
T-BONE STEAKS

*Steak doesn't get much simpler than this.
Grill the steaks or pan-sear them in a cast-iron skillet,
then finish them off with a chile-lime butter.*

Rinse and dry steaks. Place in a shallow nonreactive pan. Stir together olive oil, lime juice, and garlic. Pour over steaks, turning to coat all sides. Cover with plastic wrap and allow to come to room temperature, about 1 hour.

Remove steaks from oil and allow excess to drip off. Season steaks generously on all sides with salt and black pepper.

Meanwhile, prepare fire if grilling over coals. Coals are ready when they burn a bright red-orange. Spread coals so that there is a very hot side of the grill and a somewhat cooler area. This allows you to control the heat under the meat.

If using a cast-iron skillet, place skillet over low heat about 5 minutes before cooking to allow pan to heat through. A couple of minutes before cooking, raise heat to high. The pan should begin to smoke.

Place steaks on grill or in hot pan. Cook 3 to 6 minutes or as needed to leave char marks on the meat. Turn and char other side.

Depending on the thickness of the meat and the cooking temperature, the steak may be almost to the desired degree of doneness, preferably medium rare. If the meat seems to be getting too dark or is burning, remove to a slightly cooler area of the grill or lower heat. Cook 4 to 6 minutes longer or as desired.

Keep warm until serving time and serve on heated plates as soon as possible. Just before serving, place 1 tablespoon Chile-Lime Butter on each steak to melt.

CHILE-LIME BUTTER

In a small bowl, stir together butter, lime rind and cayenne pepper, mixing well. Place in butter molds or shape into a cylinder and wrap in wax pepper. Chill until firm. Remove from molds or slice butter into 8 1-ounce servings. Place on grilled steaks or corn.

---

4 (10- TO 12-OUNCE) T-BONE STEAKS, ABOUT 1-INCH THICK

½ CUP EXTRA-VIRGIN OLIVE OIL

¼ CUP LIME JUICE

2 CLOVES GARLIC, FINELY CHOPPED

1½ TEASPOONS SALT OR TO TASTE

2 TEASPOONS BLACK PEPPER OR TO TASTE

CHILE-LIME BUTTER

makes 4 servings

½ CUP (1 STICK) SALTED BUTTER, SOFTENED AT ROOM TEMPERATURE

1 TEASPOON GRATED LIME RIND

⅛ TEASPOON CAYENNE PEPPER OR TO TASTE

makes 8 servings

¼ CUP SUGAR

¼ CUP FIRMLY PACKED BROWN SUGAR

⅓ CUP BARBECUE SAUCE

2 TABLESPOONS KETCHUP

¼ TEASPOON SALT OR TO TASTE

1 TEASPOON BLACK PEPPER OR TO TASTE

1 TABLESPOON MOLASSES

2 TEASPOONS PREPARED MUSTARD

2 16-OUNCE CANS PORK AND BEANS,
UNDRAINED

½ CUP CHOPPED ONION

2 OUNCES CHORIZO (MEXICAN-STYLE
SAUSAGE), UNCOOKED AND CRUMBLED

8 SMALL SCALLIONS OR GREEN ONIONS,
ROOT ENDS TRIMMED

makes 8 servings

8 EARS FRESH CORN

1 LARGE POT WITH LOTS OF WATER

1 TABLESPOON SALT OR TO TASTE

½ CUP SOFT BUTTER OR SOFTENED
CHILE LIME BUTTER P. 157

makes 8 servings

COWBOY BAKED BEANS

*These are the kind of beans that would taste great in a
cast-iron Dutch oven, heated over a low fire, but a casserole
dish and an oven will do. However you heat them,
serve these baked beans with some fresh green onions.*

Preheat oven to 350°. Lightly grease a 2-quart baking dish. In a large bowl, combine sugar, brown sugar, barbecue sauce, ketchup, salt, black pepper, molasses and mustard. Stir to dissolve sugar. Add pork and beans, chopped onion and chorizo, mixing well. Pour beans into prepared dish. Bake for 1 hour, uncovered, stirring twice. Garnish each serving with a fresh green onion.

GRILLED CORN

Remove shucks from corn, rinse and pull away all the silk. Bring water to a boil over high heat. Add corn and allow water to return to the boil.

When water boils again, place a lid on the pan and turn off heat. Leave corn for 4 to 6 minutes. Remove from water, drain and lightly smear with butter. Place corn on grill over low coals just until kernels are lightly toasted, turning frequently for about 2 to 3 minutes. Par-boiling the corn makes for quicker, more even cooking.

Keep warm and serve as soon as possible.

BANANA PUDDING TRIFLE

This banana pudding that would do any black-tie-and-boots event proud.

In a 1-quart bowl, toss together bananas and lemon juice. Fold in vanilla wafers; refrigerate until ready to use. Heat milk in a medium saucepan over medium heat until simmering. Whisk in sugar, flour and salt; cook about 5 minutes, stirring frequently. Remove from heat.

Place egg yolks in a large bowl and beat until frothy. Gradually add about ½ cup of the hot milk to beaten eggs, stirring constantly. Add the egg mixture to the hot milk, stirring constantly. Return to low heat and cook until mixture is thick enough to coat the back of a wooden spoon, about 5 minutes.

Stir in vanilla.

Remove from heat and allow to cool slightly. If desired, gently mix berries into vanilla wafer-banana mixture. Pour slightly cooled custard over cookies and fruit, gently folding mixture to combine. Cover with a layer of plastic wrap directly on surface of pudding and refrigerate several hours until chilled.

Turn into a clear glass trifle dish for serving. If desired, whip cream until soft peaks form and spread over top of pudding just before servings. Garnish with additional berries, if desired.

3 RIPE BANANAS, CHILLED AND SLICED

1 TEASPOON LEMON JUICE

1 CUP BROKEN VANILLA WAFERS

2 CUPS MILK

½ TO ¾ CUP SUGAR, DEPENDING ON DESIRED SWEETNESS

1 TABLESPOON FLOUR

¼ TEASPOON SALT

2 EGGS, SEPARATED

1 TEASPOON VANILLA

1 CUP SLICED STRAWBERRIES OR BLUEBERRIES, OPTIONAL

1 CUP HEAVY CREAM, WHIPPED, OPTIONAL

makes 6 to 8 servings

2 CUPS FLOUR

¼ CUP SUGAR

1 TEASPOON SALT

2 TEASPOONS BAKING POWDER

2 TABLESPOONS SHORTENING

1 CUP WARM MILK OR WARM WATER

VEGETABLE OIL FOR FRYING

¼ CUP SUGAR

½ TEASPOON GROUND CINNAMON

HONEY

SOPAIPILLAS

*Sopaipillas are Mexican doughnuts without the hole,
similar to beignets, but more often served as a dessert.
Drizzle a hot sopaipilla with honey and watch your
resolve to eat "just one" melt away.*

In the work bowl of a food processor, combine flour, sugar, salt and baking powder using an on-off pulse motion.

Add shortening and process just until mixture looks like coarse cornmeal. Add warm water or milk gradually with processor running. It should form a stiff dough. Add a bit more flour, if needed.

Turn the dough onto a lightly floured board. Knead for 3 to 4 minutes or until dough is smooth and no longer sticky. Place in a clean, lightly oiled bowl and loosely cover with a sheet of plastic wrap and a clean dish towel.

Allow dough to rest for 30 minutes. Turn out of bowl and knead briefly for 1 to 2 minutes. Roll out dough to a thickness of ¼- to ½-inch. Cut into 2-inch squares or triangles.

Heat 2 inches of oil in a heavy saucepan to 375°. Drop 2 or 3 pieces of dough into hot oil. Fry 30 to 60 seconds, turning several times, or until puffed and golden brown. Drain on paper towels.

Combine sugar and cinnamon and sprinkle over sopaipillas. Serve immediately with honey.

makes 12 to 18 sopaipillas

BUFFALO BILL
PATRON'S BALL

In Cody, Wyoming, the cowboy formal is known as the Buffalo Bill Memorial Association Patron's Ball. Held annually to benefit the historical center and museums housing Indian and western artifacts and art, this dining-and-dancing event brings out the finest in folk, as well as their finery.

The Patron's Ball, a prime example of cowboy high style, is held in the majestic Buffalo Bill Historical Center. Many of the outfits worn to this event—fringed and beaded leather jackets and dresses, hand-tooled boots and silver jewelry—could easily be showcased in the museum. This event is formal and includes a seated dinner.

The following menu—created around dishes using native elk and trout—would dazzle Buffalo Bill. It is a feast for contemporary mountain men . . . and women.

Menu

MOUNTAIN MARTINI

PEMMICAN CONSOMMÉ WITH GARDEN VEGETABLES

SMOKED TROUT WITH BROWN SAGE BUTTER

CRUSHED BLACK PEPPERCORN ELK MEDALLIONS
WITH MUSTARD CREAM
AND BRAISED BABY VEGETABLES

MUSHROOM-STUFFED BLUE CORN CHILE RELLENOS

ROCKY MOUNTAIN COFFEE CAKE WITH FRESH PLUMS

MOUNTAIN MARTINI

*Launch a big dinner with a signature cocktail.
A Mountain Martini uses dried blue-black juniper berries
to reflect a favorite mountain flavoring—often used in
wild game dishes. And, of course, juniper is the primary
flavoring for gin. So double up on the bitter flavor by adding
juniper berries but give the martini a touch of sweet
and color with red vermouth.*

In a cocktail shaker, combine gin, vermouth and crushed ice. Shake to combine and chill; strain into a martini glass. Drop in several juniper berries and a twist of lemon.

2 OUNCES GIN

SPLASH SWEET RED VERMOUTH

CRUSHED ICE

JUNIPER BERRIES (AVAILABLE IN THE SPICE SECTION OF SPECIALTY STORES)

TWIST OF LEMON PEEL

makes 1 cocktail

PEMMICAN CONSOMMÉ *with* GARDEN VEGETABLES

This light first course draws on the frontier preservation technique that produced jerky, dehydrated meat—and pemmican, ground or shredded jerky. Plains Indians relied on venison. Cowboys favored beef, but the end result was the same: A source of protein that didn't spoil and that was light and easy to carry—plus, it made use of what was available.

In this soup, jerky is reconstituted in a delicate broth with crisp-tender vegetables, then shredded. If you don't want to make your own jerky, use only a top-quality freshly made jerky. Try to find jerky that isn't made with soy sauce so the consommé doesn't get too dark.

In a large stockpot, combine jerky and hot stock. Bring to a simmer over high heat. Simmer for 20 minutes over low heat to soften the jerky. Off heat, pick out pieces of jerky and shred it into thin strings. Return to the soup.

Meanwhile, place a medium saucepan over high heat with enough water to float the turnips, corn and leaks. When water boils, add vegetables, ½ teaspoon salt. Cook about 5 minutes, then drain.

Add blanched vegetables, tomatoes and mustard greens to soup. Taste for seasoning, adding ¼ teaspoon salt or as needed. Stir in majoram and heat through.

2 TO 3 OUNCES HOMEMADE (VENISON OR BEEF) JERKY (SEE PAGE 7) OR TOP-QUALITY PACKAGED BEEF OR VENISON JERKY

8 CUPS HOT HOMEMADE VENISON OR BEEF STOCK (SEE THE FOLLOWING RECIPE) OR USE TOP-QUALITY FROZEN OR CANNED BEEF STOCK, HEATED

⅔ CUP TURNIPS CUT INTO ¼-INCH CUBES

⅔ CUP FRESH OR FROZEN CORN KERNELS

⅔ CUP FINELY SLICED LEAK, WHITE PART ONLY

4 ROMA TOMATOES, SEEDED AND CUT INTO ¼-INCH CUBES

2 CUPS FINELY CHOPPED FRESH MUSTARD GREENS OR 1 (8-OUNCE) PACKAGE FROZEN, CHOPPED MUSTARD GREENS (THAWED AND DRAINED)

¾ TEASPOON SALT OR TO TASTE, DIVIDED USE

1 TABLESPOON FINELY CHOPPED FRESH MARJORAM OR 1 TEASPOON DRIED

makes 8 to 10 servings

3 TO 4 POUNDS BEEF OR VENISON BONES

2 TABLESPOONS BUTTER

2 TABLESPOONS CANOLA OIL

1 ONION, COARSELY CHOPPED

3 CARROTS, COARSELY CHOPPED

4 LARGE CLOVES GARLIC, CRUSHED

2 TO 3 LEEKS, COARSELY CHOPPED,
WHITE PART ONLY

1 MEDIUM TURNIP, COARSELY CHOPPED

1 CUP COARSELY CHOPPED OR SLICED
FRESH MUSHROOMS

2 CUPS DRY RED TABLE WINE

1 8-OUNCE CAN TOMATO PURÉE

1 TABLESPOON JUNIPER BERRIES,
OPTIONAL

1 TABLESPOON DRIED THYME

3 14½-OUNCE CANS BEEF STOCK

1 14½-OUNCE CAN CHICKEN STOCK

4 CANS WATER OR AS NEEDED

makes 8 cups

VENISON *or* BEEF STOCK

This is a basic broth using venison or beef.
Make up a big potful, use some and freeze the rest in
1- or 2-cup size containers so you'll have plenty at the
ready whenever a recipe calls for it.

Rinse and dry bones. In large heavy-bottom stockpot, combine butter and oil. Heat over medium heat. Add bones and cook until brown on all sides, about 10 to 15 minutes. Add onion, carrot, garlic, leek, turnip, and mushrooms. Stir and cook until vegetables are dark brown and caramelized, about 20 to 30 minutes.

Add red wine and stir to loosen any brown bits stuck to the bottom of the pan. Add tomato purée, juniper berries, and dried thyme. Raise heat to high. When liquid boils, cook until reduced to about 1½ cups.

Add stock and water; bring to a boil. Skim the liquid, reduce heat and simmer for about 2 hours until the liquid is reduced to 2 quarts (8 cups). Strain through a fine sieve or cheesecloth. Discard solids.

SMOKED TROUT *with* BROWN SAGE BUTTER

Trout from a Rocky Mountain lake or stream is one of the true joys of the high country. Lightly smoked trout bathed in brown sage butter is a sophisticated fish course.

Place a trout fillet on each serving plate. In a medium skillet, heat butter over medium heat until it bubbles and begins to turn golden brown. Add sage leaves. Stir and cook until butter and leaves are dark brown and butter smells nutty. Do not allow butter to blacken. Remove from heat immediately. Stir in salt and pepper to taste.

Allow butter to cool slightly. Pour over trout fillet and garnish each serving with a mound of tomatoes, several thin lemon slices and a couple of fresh sage leaves.

8 FILLETS OF SMOKED TROUT (AVAILABLE IN GOURMET MARKETS), ROOM TEMPERATURE

1 CUP UNSALTED BUTTER

½ TO ¾ CUP LIGHTLY PACKED FRESH SAGE LEAVES, RINSED AND DRIED

¼ TEASPOON SALT OR TO TASTE

¼ TEASPOON PEPPER OR TO TASTE

2 ROMA TOMATOES, SEEDED AND FINELY CHOPPED

2 LEMONS, VERY THINLY SLICED

FRESH SAGE LEAVES

makes 8 servings

IN THE LAST 10 YEARS, IT SEEMS LIKE EVERY MAJOR CHARITY

(IN EVERY MAJOR CITY) HAS HAD *cowboy formal* AS A THEME.

LOS ANGELES CHEF AND FUND-RAISER EXTRAORDINAIRE,

Wolfgang Puck, DOES IT. HIS THEME THE LAST COUPLE OF YEARS

HAS BEEN WESTERN NIGHT ON THE *Spartacus* (MOVIE) SET.

IT IS A BIZARRE MIX OF ROMAN AND COWBOY. EVEN *Meals* ON *Wheels*

IN NEW YORK . . . A COUPLE OF YEARS AGO, THE GALA EVENING WAS

black tie AND *blue jeans.* BUT YOU CAN ALWAYS TELL THE

DIFFERENCE BETWEEN THE REAL THING AND WHEN SOMEBODY

IS JUST DRESSED IN *cowboy attire*

FOR THE EVENING.

—*Stephan Pyles,*
founder of the Star Canyon restaurants,
Dallas and Las Vegas
author, New Texas Cuisine

CRUSHED BLACK PEPPERCORN ELK MEDALLIONS *with* MUSTARD CREAM

This recipe works equally well with any kind of venison—meaning, from any large game animal. Although venison is most often thought of as deer, the term also includes meat from moose, reindeer, caribou and antelope.

Using a tender, boneless cut, such as backstrap—similar to beef tenderloin—is preferable. Slice medallions at least 1-inch thick, allowing 3 to 4 medallions per serving, depending on size. Rinse and dry medallions, trimming to make neat round pieces.

In a shallow, nonreactive dish, combine port, beef stock, and soy sauce, stirring well. Add elk medallions, turning to coat all sides. Cover and refrigerate 8 hours, turning occasionally.

Place peppercorns on a large cutting board, lined with a layer of wax pepper. Cover with another piece of wax paper. Using the bottom of a heavy pot, a mallet or rolling pin, crush peppercorns coarsely.

Remove steaks from marinade and pat dry. Season on all sides with salt and press medallions into peppercorns to evenly coat both sides. Press peppercorns into steaks to make sure they adhere.

Heat a heavy-bottom skillet over medium-high heat. Add 2 to 3 tablespoons olive oil and 1 to 2 tablespoons butter. Cook medallions a few at a time to desired degree of doneness, preferably medium rare. Keep warm.

Add additional olive oil and butter to pan as needed and cook remaining medallions. Serve with garnish of Braised Baby Vegetables and drizzle of Mustard Cream.

---

6 TO 8 OUNCES ELK (OR OTHER VENISON) MEDALLIONS PER PERSON, CUT 1-INCH THICK

1 CUP PORT WINE

½ CUP BEEF STOCK (SEE PAGE 164) OR CANNED LOW-SALT BROTH

2 TABLESPOONS SOY SAUCE

½ CUP WHOLE BLACK PEPPERCORNS OR TO TASTE

2 TEASPOONS SALT OR TO TASTE

3 TO 6 TABLESPOONS OLIVE OIL OR AS NEEDED

2 TO 4 TABLESPOONS BUTTER OR AS NEEDED

BRAISED BABY VEGETABLES (SEE PAGE 168)

MUSTARD CREAM (SEE PAGE 168)

makes 8 servings

24 PEARL ONIONS

24 GREEN OR YELLOW BABY SQUASH
(OR A COMBINATION)

24 CHERRY TOMATOES

2 TABLESPOONS BUTTER OR OLIVE OIL,
OR A COMBINATION

½ TEASPOON SALT OR TO TASTE

makes 6 to 8 servings

2 TABLESPOONS BUTTER

2 TABLESPOONS DRY MUSTARD POWDER

¼ CUP WATER

¼ CUP HEAVY CREAM

1 TEASPOON WHITE VERMOUTH OR
TO TASTE

¼ TEASPOON SALT OR TO TASTE

makes about 1 cup

BRAISED BABY VEGETABLES

*This combination is a simple way to add color—as well
as vegetables—to a plate.*

Rinse and dry vegetables. Fill a medium saucepan about ¾ full of water. Add onions, bring to a boil over high heat and cook 1 minute. Add squash; allow water to return to a boil. Cook 1 minute longer.

Drain vegetables in a colander; plunge in a large bowl of ice water to stop cooking. Drain and set aside. Remove papery skins from onions before proceeding to next step.

In a large skillet, heat butter or olive oil over medium heat. Add onions and cook until they begin to turn golden, about 5 minutes. Add squash and cook 2 to 3 minutes longer. Add tomatoes and cook just long enough to heat through, about 2 minutes. Season to taste with salt. Use as a garnish or side dish.

MUSTARD CREAM

*An easy sauce, it works well for strong-flavored meats like
venison or on delicate fish and egg dishes.*

In a small saucepan over low heat, melt butter. Whisk in mustard powder. Add water and stir until smooth. Stir in cream and slowly bring to a simmer. Reduce heat and cook 2 to 3 minutes, stirring frequently. Add vermouth during last minute of cooking and cook just until alcohol evaporates. Add salt as needed to taste.

MUSHROOM-STUFFED BLUE CORN CHILE RELLENOS

This is a magnificent side for a cowboy banquet or a wonderful entree for a lighter cowboy sit-down.

FILLING

2 TABLESPOONS OLIVE OIL

16 OUNCES CHOPPED MUSHROOMS (USE WHITE, BROWN, SHIITAKE, CHANTERELLES, MORELS, PORTOBELLOS OR A COMBINATION)

2 CLOVES GARLIC, FINELY CHOPPED

1 LARGE SHALLOT, FINELY CHOPPED

½ CUP DRY WHITE WINE OR WHITE VERMOUTH

1 TEASPOON SALT OR TO TASTE

½ TEASPOON PEPPER OR TO TASTE

2 TABLESPOONS COARSELY CHOPPED CURLY LEAF PARSLEY OR ITALIAN PARSLEY

½ CUP CASERA (MEXICAN GOAT CHEESE)

CHILIES

8 POBLANO OR GREEN NEW MEXICO CHILIES

3 EGGS, BEATEN

3 TABLESPOONS MILK

½ CUP FLOUR

1 CUP BLUE OR YELLOW CORNMEAL (OR A COMBINATION)

VEGETABLE OIL FOR DEEP-FRYING

In a large skillet, heat olive oil over medium-high heat. Add mushrooms; stir and cook until they begin to wilt. Mix in garlic and shallot; add white wine or vermouth and cook 2 to 3 minutes longer or just until mushrooms are tender. Season to taste with salt and pepper; stir in parsley and set aside to cool. When cool, fold in cheese.

makes 8 servings

Heat broiler. Place chilies on a broiler pan and place under broiler until skins blacken and blister. Turn to blister all sides. This may take about 5 minutes.

Transfer chilies to a large, resealable plastic bag (or place in a bowl and cover tightly with plastic wrap) and let chilies steam for 15 to 20 minutes.

Carefully remove peppers from plastic and gently pull off skin using fingers or the tip of a knife. Rinse chilies under cold running water to help loosen skin. Leave stem intact.

Using a small, sharp knife, carefully slit the chile from stem end, almost to the point. Gently scrape out seeds and ribs; discard. Spoon filling into chilies, being careful not to overstuff. The chilies should be able to close completely over the stuffing; fasten with picks, if necessary.

Combine beaten eggs and milk in a shallow bowl; place flour and cornmeal in similar shallow bowls or on small plates.

Making sure chilies remain sealed, carefully roll stuffed chilies in flour to lightly coat all sides, spooning flour over chile as needed to cover evenly. Then dip into egg-milk mixture, allowing excess to drip back into bowl. After excess has dripped off, roll stuffed chilies in cornmeal, spooning cornmeal over chile as needed to cover evenly.

Pour oil in a deep saucepan or deep fryer to a depth of 2 to 3 inches. Heat oil to 350°. Gently lower a battered and stuffed chile into the oil and fry for 6 to 8 minutes or until golden and crisp. Fry a few at a time so as not to crowd fryer; sides of chilies should not touch. Drain on paper towels and keep warm until all chilies have been fried.

If desired, serve with warm red Mi Casa Salsa (see page 96) or canned tomatillo salsa and a drizzle of Mexican crema or sour cream.

ROCKY MOUNTAIN COFFEE CAKE *with* FRESH PLUMS

Served warm, this cake is a comforting dessert, especially with a scoop of ice cream or heavy cream. It can also be served as a breakfast bread.

Dissolve yeast in warm water, stirring to activate. Set aside. Heat milk until almost boiling; remove from heat. Add ½ cup sugar and ¼ cup butter. Stir to melt and allow mixture to cool to lukewarm, so as not to kill the yeast action nor cook the egg. Transfer to a medium mixing bowl.

Add dissolved yeast, egg and salt to the lukewarm milk mixture. Add flour, 1 cup at a time, mixing well after each addition. Turn out the dough onto lightly floured board. Knead for 5 to 10 minutes; dough will be sticky.

Place the dough in a lightly greased bowl, cover, and let rise in a warm place until doubled in bulk, about 1½ to 2 hours. Punch down dough and knead gently in bowl. Allow to rest for 5 to 10 minutes.

Lightly grease a 9 x 11-inch pan. Place dough on lightly floured board and roll or pat into a rectangle about ½-inch thick. Place in greased pan. Cover and let rise again until doubled, about 45 to 60 minutes. Gently pull dough to edges of pan, if dough has not filled pan during second rise.

Preheat oven to 375°. Peel fruit and cut into ½-inch slices; discard pits. You should have about 1 cup fruit. Using fingers, press slices of fruit in an attractive pattern into the dough. Melt remaining butter. Brush cake with melted butter, pressing down each piece of fruit so butter puddles. Sprinkle about 3 to 4 tablespoons sugar and cinnamon over cake, being particularly generous over fruit pieces. Drizzle cream over top of each cake, puddling cream around fruit pieces.

Bake 25 to 30 minutes or just until dough begins to brown around the edges. Cut into squares and serve warm with whipped cream or ice cream, if desired.

1 PACKAGE DRY YEAST

¼ CUP LUKEWARM WATER

¾ CUP MILK

½ CUP PLUS 3 TO 4 TABLESPOONS SUGAR

½ CUP UNSALTED BUTTER, DIVIDED USE

1 EGG, LIGHTLY BEATEN

1 TEASPOON SALT

3 CUPS FLOUR

ABOUT 1 POUND PLUMS, PEACHES OR APRICOTS

1 TO 2 TEASPOONS CINNAMON, OR TO TASTE

¼ CUP HEAVY CREAM

WHIPPED CREAM OR ICE CREAM

makes 1 cake, about 12 servings

INDEX

Italic numbers indicate photos.